MURDER IN
ROCKPORT, MASSACHUSETTS

TERROR IN A SMALL TOWN

Robert Fitzgibbon and Wayne Soini

Published by The History Press
Charleston, SC
www.historypress.com

Copyright © 2025 by Robert Fitzgibbon and Wayne Soini
All rights reserved

First published 2025

Manufactured in the United States

ISBN 9781467156318

Library of Congress Control Number: 2024950542

Notice: The information in this book is true and complete to the best of our knowledge. It is offered without guarantee on the part of the authors or The History Press. The authors and The History Press disclaim all liability in connection with the use of this book.

All rights reserved. No part of this book may be reproduced or transmitted in any form whatsoever without prior written permission from the publisher except in the case of brief quotations embodied in critical articles and reviews.

This work is dedicated with sympathy and gratitude to the surviving families of Arthur Oker and Augusta Johnson. They have not ceased to feel the pain of unhealed grief. They honor their ancestors' larger life stories, and their quest for closure motivated them to help the authors—strangers to them—to write what could be written.

*Even if we have not done what we should have,
or not been able to do what we wanted, God will forgive us.*
—*Reverend Albert M. Johanson, January 1934*

CONTENTS

Preface 9
Acknowledgements 11

1. Rockport, 1932 15
2. John E. Sullivan, Chief of Police 19
3. The Swedish Congregational Church (SCC) 21
4. Arthur Oker, Model Citizen 25
5. An Ordinary Saturday 27
6. A Terrifying Discovery 33
7. The Investigators 35
8. The Oker Murder 39
9. Rockport's Largest Funeral 43
10. The Oker Investigation 44
11. The Detectives' Dilemma 54
12. Intermission 58
13. Ada Johnson, Model Citizen 62
14. The Halloween Party 64
15. The Pyre 66
16. Torch Slayer: The Johnson Murder 68

Contents

17. The Midnight Mass	74
18. The Johnson Investigation	76
19. The Manhunt	114
20. Failure	136
21. The Hammer	140
22. A Slaughter of Swans	145
23. Aftershocks	148
24. Echoes	153
Epilogue	157
Notes	161
Bibliography	167

PREFACE

One spring morning in 1932, the inhabitants of the Massachusetts coastal town of Rockport, Massachusetts, awoke to the fear that a killer lived among them. Respected immigrant tailor and church president Arthur Oker had been beaten to death in his store on Main Street. No one knew why Oker was targeted. No one could fathom how his killer managed to escape.

On Halloween night the following year, Augusta Johnson, another immigrant affiliated with the same church as Oker, was beaten to death. Investigators believed the murders were connected, not least because a similar weapon—a hatchet or hammer—was used in both cases. Both types of tools were locally common and figure prominently in Rockport's past.

This second killing promptly led to the largest manhunt in Massachusetts State Police history up to that time. Despite an intense townwide search, neither the weapon nor the murderer were found. For decades, locals claimed to know who the killer was. But when pressed to divulge a name, they said nothing.

This book is the first comprehensive account of what became known as the "Full-Moon" or "Rockport Maniac" murders. Since no Rockport police files survive, this work reflects the authors' research into extensive contemporary newspapers, museum and library archives, interviews with locals and the few surviving state police records.

The Oker-Johnson cases were never solved or closed. They were abandoned. Armchair detectives are thus invited to pick up where the authorities left off. The authors here track the paths (including dead ends) that investigators followed in the 1930s. Come and join us.

—Robert Fitzgibbon and Wayne Soini

ACKNOWLEDGEMENTS

The authors wish to acknowledge the help of many organizations and individuals for their generous assistance during the preparation of this book. The authors also offer sincere apologies to anyone inadvertently missed.

- Robert and Sandy Burbank, The Sandy Bay Historical Society
- David Christopher Dearborn, professor of law, Suffolk University
- Katie Darling, research analyst, Massachusetts State Police
- Craig Eastland, senior law librarian, Northeastern University School of Law
- Amanda Hawk, public services manager, MIT Libraries
- Eva Korpi, translation assistance
- Chris Martin
- Andy Meyer, director of the F.M. Johnson Archives and Special Collections, Brandel Library, North Park University
- The Honorable D. Lloyd Macdonald
- Robert Ranta, president, Cape Ann Finns
- Courtney Scott Soltero
- Julie Travers, local history librarian, Sawyer Free Public Library
- Reference librarian Diane at the Boston Public Library
- The Rockport Public Library
- The Rockport Town Clerk
- Rebecca Shea, TOHP Burnham Library

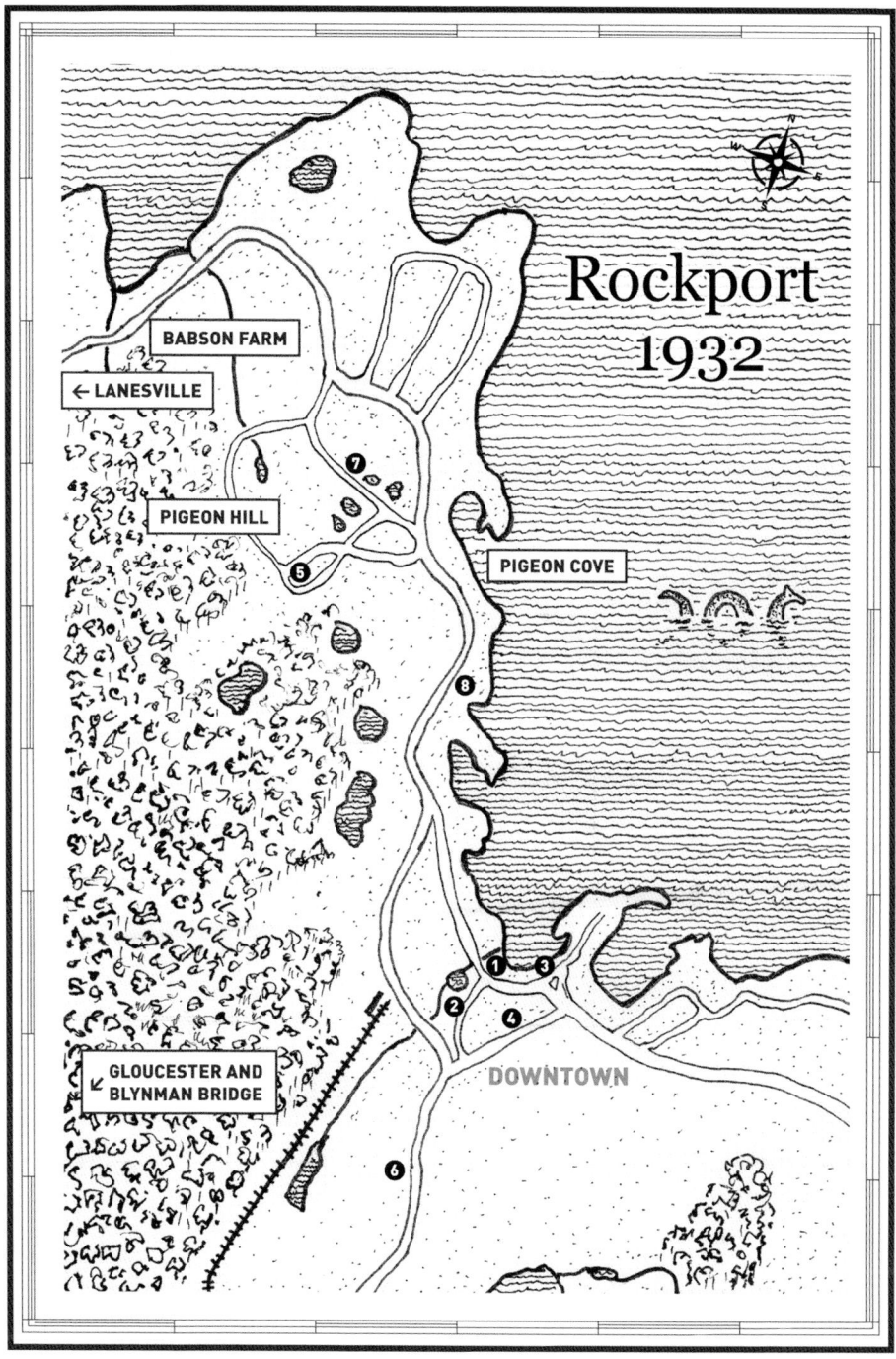

1. Oker's store
2. Oker's house
3. Rockport Police & Fire
4. Rockport Town Hall
5. Ada Johnson's house
6. Rev. Johanson's house
7. Swan house
8. Swedish Congregational Church

1

ROCKPORT, 1932

Located some twenty miles northeast of Boston, picturesque and idyllic Rockport is the tip of the Cape Ann Peninsula, a crescent-shaped town fronting the specter-haunted woods of Dogtown, its curved back bordered by the tempest-tossed Atlantic Ocean. Originally known as Sandy Bay, the town split from Gloucester and incorporated independently in 1840. If it sounds like Mayberry with a Massachusetts accent, it should:

> *A cleaner and more wholesome town in which to spend the summer cannot be found in New England. There are a number of good beaches, a beautiful shore drive, and the ocean scenery is unsurpassed. Many artists make their homes here during the summer months and find interesting subjects to transfer to their canvasses along the quaint old wharves and rugged shore.*[1]

Rockport had several distinct sections back in 1932. Downtown was located roughly between the mouth of the Mill Brook and Bearskin Neck, with Dock Square at its center. To the southwest was Broadway, which contained the library and Rockport Town Hall, a grandiose three-story wooden structure with central cathedral windows and a second-floor dance hall, the site of town meetings and socials where local women would bring freshly baked pies to auction.

To the northwest was Pigeon Cove and Pigeon Hill, the town's highest geographical point and site of multiple quarrying operations. On Pigeon Hill was the Sheep's Pasture, a rock-strewn grassland with tidy houses where the

Rockport, circa 1932. *Robert Ranta, Cape Ann Finns.*

Swedes then mostly lived. Due north was Halibut Point, a lunar landscape with panoramic views of the ocean up to the Maine coast. Due south was Long Beach. To the west was Dogtown. In colonial times, it was the center of Cape Ann, but it had been abandoned by the early 1800s and reclaimed by wild animals and forest.

Rockport, in 1932, had twelve fraternal organizations, nine churches, eight schools, three cemeteries, a hospital, a library, a post office and even a Ripley's *Believe It or Not!* house made entirely of paper by an engineer who designed paper clip manufacturing machines for a living. Monied summer residents and flighty artists came each summer for the scenery. The Rockport Selectmen were plumber Ralph T. Parker (chair), John H. Dennis and realtor Roy H. Lane. Frederick H. Tarr Jr. was the town's attorney and a state representative, son of U.S. Attorney Frederick H. Tarr.

Rockport society was a tiered layer cake: the old-money and some-money Yankees on top, the Irish in the middle and the immigrants on the bottom—in Rockport, the immigrants were mostly Swedes and Finns. Swedish immigrants started coming to Cape Ann in the 1870s, settling in the Pigeon Hill section of Rockport. The men worked in the granite quarries, and the women worked as domestic servants. Finnish immigrants came soon after, settling on Forest Street (aka "Finn Alley") and Lanesville, a section of Gloucester due west of Pigeon Cove. The Yankees saw the Swedes as wholesome, industrious and aligned with the Anglo-Saxon values of the nation. The Finns, brought to the quarries as strike-breakers and subsequently gaining some reputedly "bolshie" socialist leanings, not so much. They were seen as clannish, a bit mysterious. Both Swedes and Finns experienced challenges in their new land—social isolation, economic difficulties and learning a new language—but were assimilating.

However, Rockport's year-round population had plummeted from 4,500 in 1910, 3,630 in 1930 and down to an estimated 3,500 in 1932. The Depression, on top of the collapse of the granite industry, had done a number on the town. The deep quarries that once provided stones for building and paving blocks for roads from New Hampshire to Virginia now sat idle and abandoned. Businesses operated at fractional capacity and made do with part-time or "on-call" workers.

Rockporters were barely scraping by. In 1930, one hundred residents registered at town hall for local aid. The same year, to relieve homeowning taxpayers, Rockport trimmed its tax rate back to 1923 levels. In 1932, school employees were required to give back 5 percent of their salary to cover the town's welfare costs. There were cases of diphtheria among children. The town organized unemployed male citizens into labor gangs to dig ditches and plant trees to qualify for relief and get the government handouts of grapefruit, lard and coal. The Red Cross delivered emergency flour.

Vagrants arrived in town looking for work, only to be run out or arrested. Juvenile delinquency was up in town, on Cape Ann, in Massachusetts—heck, across the entire nation. Who knew that between real desperation and the pre-code gangster movies, the reputation the Greatest Generation first earned was that they were lawless hellions?

Fortunately, there was not much violent crime in Rockport. The one event that stood out was when John Dinn, upset that he ran for selectman in March 1930 and received not a single vote, took an axe and demolished his own house on High Street in a frenzy, littering the road with smashed furniture and splintered wood. It took multiple officers to subdue Dinn enough to have him wrapped in a straitjacket and sent to the state hospital. More frequently, people in town went crazy quietly.

The Rockport Police Department occupied the same building as the volunteer fire department downtown at 3 Dock Square. Its walls were decorated with paintings donated by visiting artists. There was a single holding cell. The department had a single patrol car and one Harley-Davidson motorcycle. There were twenty-two part-time "special police" and constables, who were especially needed during the crowded summer tourist months. There were only four full-time officers. Officer Andrew Stevens, age seventy-seven, had the official title of janitor of lockup. There was also Officer John V. Spates. Above him was James T. "Jimmy" Quinn, who, as motorcycle officer, got to ride the chopper; unofficially, he was curator of the department's art collection.

2
JOHN E. SULLIVAN, CHIEF OF POLICE

At the top, earning an annual salary of $1,842.50, was Chief John E. Sullivan. The most venerable of town fathers, Rockport native John Sullivan became a special officer in 1890 and a regular officer in 1894, back when Rockport was rough and tumble—stabbings at the Socialist Hall on Squam Hill, labor strikes among the Nordic immigrant quarry workers, sailors on a drunk and larcenies against the tourists at the Straitsmouth Inn. He made a name for himself, throwing a few punches of his own. He even lost a thumb, bitten off by an "insane" Lanesville Finn while getting arrested. But he wasn't all mean. Patrolling the railroad yard, Sullivan would meet incoming immigrants and check them out while offering directions through sign language or maps hand drawn on the spot. He was often remembered by immigrant families for his warm welcome and courtesy during their first hour in Rockport, when America was overwhelming, new and confusing.

John Sullivan, Rockport police chief. *From the Gloucester Daily Times/ North of Boston Media Group.*

Back then, Rockport citizens would elect "constables," who would then be appointed policemen by the selectmen, with their yearly term beginning May 1. In 1900, Sullivan was elected constable at a town meeting, but the selectmen refused to appoint him to the force. In turn, Sullivan got himself elected to the newly created title of chairman of the constables and, as such, patrolled the streets as a "citizen's police."

By 1904, Sullivan was the chief of police, a post he retained thereafter continuously until 1922, when selectmen refused to reappoint him chief. A fresh crop of selectmen reappointed Sullivan the next year, and each board thereafter did the same. In his dark blue uniform with gold buttons and badge, Sullivan had his power base, knew everyone in town, held sway at town meetings and had a reputation for his "clever work" as a policeman, knowing what to press and what to let slide:

> *They used to gamble at Howard Hodgkin's fishing shack all the time, nickels and dimes, I suppose. But now and then a woman would call up the police and complain. So one day some woman…complained to Chief Sullivan and said, "There's gambling going on down there in Howard Hodgkin's fish shack, and if you don't do something about it I'm going to see John Henry Dennis* [a selectman and town moderator]*." Sullivan said he'd take care of it right away. So he picked up the phone and called Howard and said, "Howard, I've had a complaint that somebody's down there playing cards; now I don't believe it, but I want you to know that I'm coming right down to investigate." When he got down there, they were reading the Bible to each other. So he reported back…that he had found no gambling and that it must have been an ugly rumor somebody started.*[2]

Through many years and many winks and nods, the long-term chief exercised an easy control over his small department in his small town, a quiet place with a bit of a margin.

3

THE SWEDISH CONGREGATIONAL CHURCH (SCC)

Upon arrival, Rockport's Swedish and Finnish immigrants set up their own houses of worship. The Finns founded Lutheran churches in Lanesville and Rockport. The Swedes set up not one but three separate denominations in Rockport. These multiple churches (two on the same street) make contemporary and modern references to "the Swedish church in Rockport" imprecise and confusing. Organizationally and on a personal level, these church denominations did not get along. But the church that figures prominently in this story was the Swedish Congregational Church (SCC).[3]

The SCC was the most evangelical of the three Swedish churches in Rockport. Its precursor was the Swedish Evangelical Mission Church, formed in January 1892 by eleven immigrants whose "free church" doctrinal views on atonement and membership differed greatly from the state-sponsored Lutheran Church back home. On a democratic foundation of lay preachers and self-government, the group grew to thirty-five members within a year. They held crowded meetings at the home of Olof Moody, half-jokingly styled "Moody Hall" on Granite Street near the Rockport Granite Company.

In 1894, the congregation built a simple but elegant wooden structure, painted white, at 111 Granite Street. In 1895, it combined with the Congregational Fellowship to become the Swedish Evangelical Congregational Church. In 1897, the Council of Congregational Churches granted official recognition to this Rockport outpost as the Swedish Congregational Church (Mission Covenant, aka Missions Vanner).

In 1908, a Ladies Aid Society began its active role in raising funds for orphanages, missionary work in China and the Scandinavian Sailors Home in East Boston. A Young People's Society began in the mid-1920s to encourage Christian behavior among the youth and to assist the pastor. Sunday School attendance in 1929 was a record-breaking forty.

The year 1932 saw the fortieth anniversary of the SCC, which had grown into a small but vibrant community, the last place one would expect sin to crouch by the door. Not all churchgoers were members; fewer than half committed to the church, pledged tithes and "signed the book." The minister reported:

> *At the last annual meeting, the congregation consisted of 40 members. At the 4 funerals that I was called to serve since I arrived here, we have seen hundreds of Swedes gathering. And at our Christmas morning sermon, the church was full, even the small hall, to the last pew.*[4]

On Sundays, morning and evening services were conducted in Swedish and English, plus Sunday school and the Young People's Meeting. There were prayer meetings on Thursdays.

Singing was a passion and strength of the SCC. There was an adult choir, a junior choir with sixteen voices, holiday concerts and soloists accompanied by organ or piano, and the church would host visiting musicians like the Male Chorus of the Lutheran Bible School of Grand Forks, North Dakota. It also held the typical schedule of fairs and bazaars.

The SCC's church leaders reflected ethnic unity, but there was class diversity. The pastor was the tall, thin Albert M. Johanson, formerly of Brooklyn and Minnesota, who was hired by the church in November 1931; his wife, Helen, was both his life and church partner who managed the vital choir and music programs, plus the Young People's Society. The couple had recently celebrated their silver wedding anniversary. The pastor emeritus was Reverend J. Waldemar Harrald, relocated from East Boston. The church auditors were Mrs. John Lilja and Olof (Elof) Olson, a paving cutter. Miss Blanche Carne, the teenage daughter of Pigeon Hill's William and Susie Carne, was the organist. Glue worker Herman Larson was a trustee and vice secretary; Carl Strandhal, whose three girls were Rockport schoolteachers, was a trustee and church caretaker; quarry foreman Charles Johnson was another trustee. Mrs. Robert Stillman was the treasurer, thirty-three-year-old carpenter John S. Lilja was the financial secretary and paving cutter Axel Anderson was the secretary.

Swedish Congregational Church. *Robert Fitzgibbon*.

The vice president and Sunday school superintendent was Swedish-born August (Per) Olson, a stonecutter for Ames Monuments in Lynn. A strict and religious man, the forty-six-year-old Olson had been an SCC member since 1903 and had run the Sunday school since 1925. His wife, Sigrid, was the vice secretary and a flower committee member of the Ladies Aid Society. Their second son, Melvin, was a straight-A student and former treasurer of the Young People's Society; he graduated from Rockport High School in June 1932 and attended Harvard University the following fall.

Their eldest son, Warren, blond and short like his father, was still home and a large presence in the church community. The nineteen-year-old Warren didn't drink, smoke, chase girls or go to movies. He read the Bible daily, served as a church usher, sang as a soloist in the youth choir and was vice president of the Young People's Society. Warren worked as a clerk in a local grocery store to help raise money for his brother's tuition. Most Rockporters would have described Warren as a great kid; his father described him as a "pure soul."[5]

The last and perhaps most prominent church leader had been an SCC member for decades and had previously served as a deacon, Sunday school head and financial secretary. President since 1929 and recently re-elected by unanimous vote in January, he was the father of four and the owner-operator of a profitable tailor shop on Main Street.

His name was Arthur Oker.

4
ARTHUR OKER, MODEL CITIZEN

Arthur Felix Oker was born on December 7, 1874, in Nurmijärvi, Finland, but grew up in Ekenäs, a town with a large ethnic Swedish population. Although he was born in Finland, Oker's ancestry was Swedish or possibly "mustalainen" (Finnish gypsy). Little is known of his boyhood or youth other than he married another Finnish ethnic Swede, Ida Emilia Lindervall, on May 14, 1896. He was twenty-one; she was twenty-three. They immediately started having children.

In 1904, Arthur Oker immigrated alone to America, settling in Titusville, Pennsylvania. He then sent for his family. Ida Oker and their three children immigrated through Ellis Island in 1905, but there was a mix-up with the train. After traveling two hundred miles in the wrong direction, Ida and the children eventually made it to Titusville, but the ordeal traumatized her. She was most comfortable within her immigrant community but forever timid and fearful in the larger American world.

The family settled in Rockport in 1907 and continued having children— eight in total, four of whom survived to

Mr. and Mrs. Arthur Oker. *From the collection of Ola and Mary Pearson; courtesy of Mary K. Curran.*

adulthood. Arthur worked as a tailor, Ida as a seamstress. Arthur and Ida joined the SCC in 1908, with membership numbers 112 and 113. Arthur opened his shop downtown. They rented and eventually purchased their cute, elm-shaded, three-story Victorian at 109 Main Street.

The Oker family was unique in the respect that, as Swedish Finns, they straddled both of Rockport's Nordic immigrant communities. It was also exceptional in the fact that Arthur, as a tailor and small businessman, had gained a foothold in the American middle class, while many of his immigrant peers were part of the working class. The trilingual Arthur and his children had a wide and close circle of friends across all of Rockport's population.

By 1932, Arthur Oker was fifty-seven years old, an honest and respectable man of medium height and build. His eyes were blue behind wire-framed glasses. He had a mustache and prominent bald head with a fringe of light brown hair. His family had grown and evolved. His son Arthur Jr., then thirty, was out of the house, a mechanic in Flint, Michigan. Arne, then twenty-seven, was a commercial artist in Southbridge. Rudolph, then twenty-one, a chauffeur, still lived on the second floor of his parents' home. On the first floor lived their attractive daughter Ellie; her husband, intrepid tugboat Captain Roger Martin; and their seven-year-old son, Roger. The boy would later reminisce about Arthur's bristly kisses and the surprise lollipops he would hide for his grandson in the spaces between the couch cushions as his wife and daughter gaily chatted in Swedish.

5
AN ORDINARY SATURDAY

May 21, 1932

8:00 a.m.

On the cool and cloudy day after the Flower Moon, Arthur Oker entered Oker's Tailor and Haberdashery Shop at 77 Main Street a little after 8:00 a.m. to start his workday. Saturdays were usually busier than any weekday as customers ran in and out for fittings and to check on orders, try things on and buy goods that Oker displayed in his window, like men's ties and fashion accessories.

The shop was located a little north of downtown on the ocean side of Main Street at the corner of Beach Street. The rear of the property faced Front Beach and the Atlantic Ocean. Out front, flanking the main door, were two display windows that jutted out into the sidewalk; they were filled with new suits and items of clothing, tastefully arranged. Above the door and windows was a scalloped canvas awning. The main wooden door was itself mostly window, with a fabric shade on a roller. Oker rolled the shade up. The store was open for business.

77 Main Street today. *Robert Fitzgibbon.*

9:30 A.M.

Walter Korpi of Granite Street came into the store and purchased a suit for five dollars down.

10:00 a.m. (Estimated)

Mr. Oker received a phone call. The number rang at both his shop and his home. Mrs. Oker answered but hung up when she heard her husband at his store speaking to someone on the line. Mrs. Oker did not speak English well and did not understand their conversation. The call lasted up to twenty minutes.

10:00–10:15 a.m.

Mr. Melvin Linder, twenty-seven, entered the shop. A Pigeon Cove local, Linder worked at the General Electric plant in Lynn. He came to get alterations made on a new suit he had recently purchased in Gloucester. It is unclear if Oker had finished his call by the time Linder entered or if Linder overheard any of the conversation. But a few minutes after entering, Linder noticed a man in a new straw or felt hat and a brown topcoat coming downstairs from the upstairs bathroom. The man was about five feet, ten inches tall, 150 pounds, light complexioned with blond hair and in his mid-twenties. The straw-hatted man entered the main area. The man sat in a chair near the end of the counter on the eastern side of the store, opposite of Linder and Oker as the two discussed the alterations and Mr. Oker took measurements. The man with the straw hat stared out the back window and said not a word.

Miss Margaret Allen of School Street entered the store to pick up a dress that she had ordered to be cleaned. She saw two men in the store with Oker. She saw black-haired Mr. Linder. Mr. Linder glanced at her. He was trying a coat on, facing a mirror to her left.

Linder said, "It doesn't fit."

To her right, the other man was seated in a chair behind the counter. Oker stood between the two, facing Linder. The straw-hatted man remained silent, apparently deep in thought and paying no attention to the fitting. Both men appeared in their thirties. She knew neither of them. She did not get a good look at their faces. Miss Allen paid one dollar, quickly picked up her dress and left the store.[6]

11:00 a.m.

A&P manager George Moors saw Oker step outside the front door of his shop around this time, look around, up and down the street, and then re-enter his shop.

11:10 A.M.

Mrs. Eva Dorothy from across the street observed a six-foot-tall man in a topcoat and straw hat enter the store.[7]

11:15 A.M. (ESTIMATED)

Melvin Linder left Oker's store.

11:20 A.M.

Postman Ralph Wilson entered Oker's shop to drop off an insured, registered mail package. It was eighteen inches square, three inches deep and soft and light to the touch, consistent with a bolt of cloth. Wilson, a married man and World War I veteran, knew everyone in town. He recalled two strangers with Oker. One man, red-headed, light-complexioned and looking "like a Swede," was trying on a suit and turned his face away when Wilson entered.[8] The other man was seated. Wilson could see only his profile. Wilson had a hard time describing either of the men later. He thought they might have been seafarers, as both seemed to be wearing sailor suits. In any case, Oker signed for the package, and the postman left the store.

11:30 A.M.

Rockport lobsterman and Straitsmouth Lighthouse keeper Hoyt Smith came to the shop to purchase a pair of woolen socks. He was out of luck. The front door was locked, the window shade drawn. He had a brief conversation on the street with Mrs. Viola Frasier, who was waiting for the 11:35 a.m. bus to Gloucester.

11:45 A.M.

Twelve-year-old Merrill (Merton) Mclane tried the door of the tailor shop. The door was locked, the shades drawn.

11:50 A.M.

Mrs. Oker called her husband at the shop. She wanted items from the A&P grocery store next door. He did not answer.

11:55 a.m.

Building landlord Samuel Henderson noticed that Oker's front door shade was drawn. He tried the door but found it locked. Henderson didn't think much of it. Oker typically went home at noon for lunch. He assumed that Oker had pulled the shade down to let people know he was out.

Mrs. Oker again called her husband at the shop. He did not pick up the phone.

Main Street was crowded with shoppers on both sides of the broad thoroughfare. A man named Maurice rode his bicycle to Oker's shop. He was there to pick up a pair of trousers he had altered. The door was locked, the shade drawn. He heard no sound inside. Maurice pedaled away.

12:05 p.m.

Mrs. Oker called the shop a third time. Mr. Oker did not pick up the phone.

12:15 p.m.

Mrs. Oker telephoned her husband a final time. It wasn't like him to be late for lunch. In the decades he had owned his store, he was always home by noon. She told her son Rudolph, who was out chopping wood in the backyard, to go down to the A&P, pick up some fixings for lunch and check on his father. Both stores were not far away, one-tenth of a mile at most, less than six hundred feet. It was perhaps a three-minute walk at most for a young man. Rudolph set off for downtown.

12:28 p.m.

Rockport Police jailkeeper Andrew Stevens left his home at 1 Mill Lane to board the 12:35 p.m. bus to Gloucester. He stopped at Oker's to look at a shirt and tie in the display window. He had previously told Oker that he would swing by to purchase them. But he saw the shade was drawn down on the main door. He tried the door. It was locked.

Robert Kline, who ran the Rockport Dye House two doors down from Oker's, saw Stevens at the door of the tailor shop.

Stevens was curious and peered inside the shop. Items and signs in the display area blocked his vision. He could not see well because of the clutter. The interior of the store was dark. It looked like Oker, who was standing behind the counter with his hands resting on it, was in conversation with a man who was standing at the front of the counter. The man, with his back turned toward Stevens, was wearing a light tan suit or maybe a light brown topcoat and a straw hat.

Stevens walked to the bus stop two doors east. He noticed a nearby display clock read 12:30 p.m. The Gloucester bus arrived. Officer Stevens hopped aboard. The bus drove away.

12:35 p.m. (Estimated)

Rudolph Oker arrived at his father's shop. The door was locked. The green door shade was drawn. Rudolph turned and looked up Main Street and down Beach Street—maybe his father was about—but he didn't see him. Rudolph walked up Main Street as far as the L.E. Smith Building.[9] Rudolph returned to his father's building. He tried the door to his father's shop again. It was still locked.

12:35–12:45 p.m. (Estimated)

Rudolph made his purchases at the A&P. He went back next door. The shade was still drawn, the door locked. Rudolph rushed home and dropped off the groceries. He told his mother the door was locked, and she gave him a duplicate key. He went back to the store. He unlocked the door.

12:50 p.m.

At the Rockport Police Station, Chief Sullivan got a phone call.

6

A TERRIFYING DISCOVERY

Saturday, May 21, 1932

12:55–1:15 p.m.

As he was about to open the locked door with the spare keys, Rudolph briefly said hello to Eben (Benjamin) Green, who was passing by on his way back from the post office. Green hadn't gone more than fifty yards farther when he saw Rudolph run out, screaming at him to come back because something terrible had happened to his father. Green came in and phoned the police. Hearing the commotion, landlord Sam Henderson came in and told them to call the doctor.

Patrolman John V. Spates was the first responder to arrive at the emergency at 77 Main Street. Rudolph Oker, behind the counter, was attending to his father, who was unconscious and lying face down in a still-widening puddle of blood. His glasses and false teeth were beside him. The back of his skull was, to use a nautical term common in this seaside village, "stove in," with a bone fracture line extending down the man's bulging forehead. Both his pinky fingers were practically severed from each of his hands, futile defensive wounds. He was still breathing—barely.

Dr. Ezra E. Cleaves, who lived just down the street, arrived at the shop. He, in turn, made an emergency call for the Gloucester Police ambulance. Rockport Policeman Frank Allen arrived on the scene. Gloucester Patrolman

Ralph A. Levie drove the ambulance, accompanied by an unnamed Gloucester Police officer to downtown Rockport. The four officers hustled Arthur Oker's body into the vehicle. Levie sped away, with Officer Allen riding along.

12:55–1:05 p.m. (Estimated)

Oker succumbed to his wounds in the ambulance. That day's edition of the *Gloucester Daily Times* claimed, perhaps sentimentally, that Oker expired just as the vehicle was passing Our Lady of Good Voyage Church downtown on its way toward Addison Gilbert Hospital.

Rockport Chief Sullivan briefly stopped at Oker's tailor shop and then drove to Addison Gilbert, only to hear that Oker had died.

Sullivan was a man in his seventies at the height of his professional wisdom, popularity and power. In April, the Rockport Selectmen had appointed him for the thirty-second time as police chief. He had, at the time, received accolades and well-wishes from fellow citizens, law-enforcement officers, current and former district attorneys and superior court justices. For decades, he kept Rockport's citizens safe and maintained a level of calm in an otherwise sleepy community. But this was a situation that he, in his long years of public service, had never encountered. Sullivan placed a call to the Massachusetts State Police and to the Essex County District Attorney's Office in Salem.

It was the first murder in Rockport in fifty-five years.

7
THE INVESTIGATORS

Murder Investigations in 1930s Massachusetts

Murders are cases apart. If someone takes a life, it is instantly a matter for municipal, county and state law enforcement personnel. This account covers the activities of three separate law-enforcement agencies: the Rockport Police Department, the Essex County District Attorney's Office and the Massachusetts State Police. An explanation about each organization and how they worked together may be useful.

The Rockport Police is the law enforcement organization for the Town of Rockport, which is part of Essex County in the state of Massachusetts.

A district attorney (or DA) for a county is an elected official who represents the government and serves as the prosecuting officer in criminal cases. The DA has an office in the county seat near the courthouse (for Essex County, this is in Salem) and a small staff and deputies (assistant district attorneys who do much of the day-to-day casework).

With a capital crime such as homicide, the DA would take an active role to coordinate the investigation and, depending on locale, might opt to direct it. Since Rockport was a small town with a tiny police force inexperienced in murder cases, the DA's office ran the investigation.

Attached to the DA's office was one or more detectives, who would assist the DA in investigating crimes. Although these detectives worked in and for the DA's office, they were part of the Inspections Branch of the state police.

If necessary, the DA could call upon the resources of the Massachusetts State Police headquarters at the state house in Boston, e.g. additional detectives or technical specialists such as photographers, ballistics and fingerprint experts. Another resource could be "Staties," the uniformed state troopers. These resources would supplement the existing two detectives who were paid by the state and worked out of the DA's office in Essex County exclusively.

Essex County District Attorney Hugh Cregg

Born in Lawrence, the sandy-haired, ruddy-complexioned Cregg was a star athlete at his local high school before attending Phillips Exeter Academy and the University of Vermont. He graduated from Boston University Law School in 1912 and then practiced law in Methuen.

He pivoted to a political career in 1920, becoming state senator for the Fifth Essex District from 1921 to 1929. His big impact as a senator came in 1928, when he chaired a committee investigating allegations that legislators had held a "wild party" in the state house and that members of the Massachusetts Department of Public Safety had improperly diverted confiscated liquor. A fiscal penny-pincher and conservative Catholic, Cregg was a member of the Holy Name Society, a laity confraternity dedicated to fighting immorality.

District Attorney Hugh Cregg. *Alton H. Blackington Collection, Robert S. Cox Special Collections and University Archives Research Center, UMass Amherst Libraries.*

Republican Cregg defeated John A. Costello for Essex County's district attorney seat in 1930. Cregg was still new in his DA tenure but was a consummate politician and tight with other politicos up and down the Massachusetts political scene.

The DA's team included Assistant DAs Charles Green and John E. Wilson, plus two state police detectives.

State Detective Lieutenant William F. Murray

Son of Irish immigrants, Murray served fourteen years in the Lynn Police Department, rising through the ranks from patrolman to inspector. He joined the state police constabulary in 1912 and was assigned to the Essex County DA's office in 1914. By 1931, he was a respectable property owner with five kids and a wife, his gray hair no doubt an outcome of his deep experience with scores of crimes, including murder.

State Detective Lieutenant Richard Griffin

Another son of Irish immigrants, six-foot-two-inch-tall Richard Griffin graduated high school in 1898 to a life as a heel burnisher in the shoe factories of Haverhill. After a half-dozen years on the factory floor, Griffin got a break from a fellow Fenian to join the city's police force, working as a beat cop until 1922, when he joined the Massachusetts State Police. Within a few years, he'd worked his way up to detective and got assigned to the Essex County DA's Office. Griffin, a devout Catholic with a golfing habit, still lived in his hometown with a wife and two boys.

Tall, thin Griffin and stout Murray frequently worked as a team. In 1931, they were transferred from the DA's Salem office to the Detectives Branch at the state house, which, knowing Cregg, probably was an administrative cost-cutting move, as they continued to work with Cregg on Essex County cases.

Two more detectives will join us later in the book:

State Detective Lieutenant Joseph Louis Ferrari

The son of Italian immigrants, Boston-born Joseph Louis (aka Giuseppe Luigi) joined the fire department in 1905 and switched over to the police force in 1909. He quickly became a star detective, solving twenty murders in little over a decade. In 1921, Ferrari asked to join the state police detective force, a request that required the approval of Boston Police Commissioner Curtis and Mayor Peters. Ferrari became the first Italian American in the Massachusetts State Police. Ferrari's reputation continued to grow, and he became known, with his colleagues Stokes, Sherlock and Fleming, as part of the "Four Aces," super-sleuths of the force.

State Police Detective Lieutenant Michael J. Barrett

Another Haverhill Police and State Constabulary veteran, Barrett had deep experience working cases in Suffolk and Middlesex County, often traveling to distant cities like New Orleans to bring fugitives to justice. Detective Barrett was also one of three instructors at the state police school.

The Massachusetts State Police

The Massachusetts legislature created a state police constabulary in 1865. It continued through subsequent decades as a small and rather informal force until 1919, when state legislators created a new Department of Public Safety and Governor Coolidge appointed Alfred F. Foote as the state's first commissioner. Foote proposed a massive department reorganization, and Governor Channing Cox signed the legislation to create the Massachusetts State Police in 1921.

A career army professional, Foote rose through the ranks from private to colonel, serving in the Spanish-American War and the Mexican Border Campaign. In World War I, Foote commanded the 104th Infantry Division, fighting at Belleau Wood. Unsurprisingly, Foote created a police force modeled on his military experience. It consisted of three departments:

- The uniformed state police patrol under an executive officer.
- The Inspections Branch of plainclothes detectives and specialists under the chief of inspections.
- A Fire Prevention Division under the state fire marshal.

The uniformed branch was a militarized monastic order. Troopers patrolled state roads via motorcycle, horseback or patrol car. They were deliberately assigned to posts far from their hometowns, living in barracks. Tours of duty consisted of ten consecutive days of work, followed by a twenty-four-hour period off. Uniforms were First World War castoffs, but by the summer of 1933, they had been replaced by the iconic "French and electric blue" two-tone military-style uniform with jodhpurs and a peaked cap.

By the early 1930s, the state police comprised 20 fire inspectors, 260 uniformed troopers and 26 detectives, with access to photographers, a ballistics expert and a chemist.

8

THE OKER MURDER

Saturday, May 21, 1932

1:15–11:59 p.m.

Chief Sullivan returned to Oker's store. Sullivan and Officers Spates and Quinn did a quick sweep of the building's interior. They found no one hidden on the premises and no signs of forced entry.

A little after 2:00 p.m., State Police Detective William Murray arrived. The official investigation could begin. Detective Murray and Chief Sullivan canvassed for witnesses.

They began by asking Rudolph Oker about what happened. Rudolph mentioned that his father was always punctual in coming home for lunch. When he didn't show up at home, Rudolph went to check on him. Oker had suffered unspecified bouts of illness in the past, so Rudolph and his mother wanted to make sure that Mr. Oker was all right. Police speculated that had Rudolph had the spare key with him at 12:30 p.m., he might have interrupted the assault. The police dismissed Rudolph, promising to be in touch. Rudolph went home to break the terrible news to his mother and sister, telephone his brother in Southbridge and send a telegram to his other brother in Flint.

The investigators studied the crime scene. At the front of the shop was the store; the rear was where Oker did his tailoring work. There was a back entrance that led to a yard. The door was locked from the inside, possibly with a key in the mechanism; there appeared to be no way someone could leave by the back door and then lock it. That implied the killer had left the store using the front door after setting the spring lock to secure it behind them. The killer did not leave through the back window. There was dust on the inside windowsills.

The officers inspected the front door shade. It had been pulled down with some force. The shade fabric was ripped from some of the staples that attached it to the roller. Detached, someone had secured the torn part between the door and the roller to keep it up.

The main area of the store was in shambles. A six-foot burlap screen lay toppled in a corner. A small ironing board, used to iron men's sleeves, was also on the floor. Clothing on the workbench was in disarray. The counter was covered in crumpled wax paper. Blood splatters were everywhere, spoiling the merchandise and leaving graceful, drying arcs on the furniture and walls above the clothing racks. There was a large pool of blood by the sewing machine.

Given Oker's wounds, the Rockport Police and Detective Murray speculated that he was attacked from behind. In a terrific struggle, it appeared that Oker made his way through the room, knocking stuff over, and ran behind the counter, where he was hit multiple times with a heavy, blunt yet sharp object. Bending over the counter, he raised his hands to protect his head and suffered wounds to his fingers, with the pinkies of both hands nearly severed. Bloody smears marred the crinkled packing paper, perhaps implying his hands were flailing as he was bent over. Oker then collapsed.

On the floor behind the counter was a small safe. The door of the safe was slightly ajar, with an inch of space between the door and the safe jamb. The officers opened the safe. There was blood on the interior of the door and the floor of the safe—accounts differ about whether there were droplets or a puddle of blood. But there were no bills. Inside the safe, Patrolman Quinn found a small, unbloodied hammer. It was not the murder weapon. There was also the stub of a lottery ticket. A clump of hair was stuck to a corner; the *Boston Herald* reported that it was black and gray hair, not from Oker's head.[10]

On the floor next to the safe was an oblong box, part of the safe equipment and perhaps where Oker kept his cash. There was an insignificant amount of small change inside.

Reviewing the merchandise, the investigators wondered if a topcoat was missing. The investigators found a light gray vest hanging on a rack about nine feet from where Oker's body lay. It was tucked away, hanging on a coat hanger, sandwiched between a couple of coats. It was also stained with a couple drops of blood. Perhaps it was due to an errant blood splatter—the universe can be so random.

Or perhaps the killer swapped out some of his own bloody clothing for the merchant's wares.

They noted that Officer Spates found Oker with his pockets turned out and his car and store keys and billfold missing. But given there were only three or four customers that morning, he couldn't have earned much cash. Still, robbery was a possible motive.

Officers Quinn and Allen removed every single article from the shelves in the store, looking for the murder weapon. Whatever the weapon was, it was not there. But Oker's heavy tailor shears were missing.[11]

On the counter were the day's receipts and appointments book. In the indexed notebook, Detective Murray noticed that a line under the letter *D* had been erased. Perhaps Oker wrote the killer's name down during the transaction, and the killer erased it before he left. Murray confiscated the book as evidence to send the state police crime lab. Perhaps chemicals could lift out the erased entry and render it legible.

State Detective Richard Griffin and Assistant DA Charles Green arrived in the early evening. They surveyed the crime scene, and then the police secured the premises; the investigation continued at the police station. The plan was to interview witnesses and assess potential suspects. They expected to work long past midnight.

Police interviewed a witness across the street from Oker's shop who claimed they saw a tall man in a brown topcoat and a straw hat leaving Oker's premises sometime just after 12:30 p.m. The witness could not describe the man's face, as his head was bowed down while he was walking away.[12] Catching wind of Postman Wilson's story, Chief Sullivan interviewed two local employees of the Charlestown Navy Yard, both of whom provided solid alibis.

Under the orders of the DA, Dr. Ira Hull performed the autopsy on Oker at the Burgess Funeral Home at 12 Prospect Street in Rockport. As the official witness, Officer Frank Allen stood in the antiseptic tile room, impassively watching. Dr. Hull poked and prodded, sliced and weighed, giving official descriptions of Mr. Oker's corporal violations. The face was unmarked, but the left eye and ear were discolored, the right eye shut. There were at least five and up to thirteen cuts on the top front part of the head—the number reported seemed to increase with each newspaper edition—with the back of the skull savagely crushed in with open holes in the cranium. There were otherwise no marks from blows to the face. In Oker's right hand was a needle, which had pierced the palm of his hand. The coroner reported that the deceased had clearly met his death by violence.

Although Oker's tailor shears were missing from the premises, his wounds were more consistent with those made by a hammer or hatchet. Given his injuries, Oker would have survived thirty minutes at most, which placed the time of his attack around 12:30 p.m., sometime between the visits of Policeman Stevens and Oker's son Rudolph.

Waves lapped the shore of Front Beach. Crowds lined the sidewalk outside the crime scene, whispering and peering into its darkened windows. They stayed late into the night. Down the street in their home, Oker's wife and daughter clutched each other and wept.

9
ROCKPORT'S LARGEST FUNERAL

Tuesday, May 24, 1932
2:00 p.m.

Reverend Albert M. Johanson presided over Arthur Oker's funeral at the Swedish Congregational Church. The closed-casket service was given in English and Swedish. Assisting Johanson was J.W. Harrald, the church's previous pastor, along with Reverend Frederick Pamp of Boston and Reverend Samuel Ronka of Lanesville. Reverend Johanson spoke of the fine qualities of the deceased, how Oker himself had addressed the congregation from that very pulpit as a lay preacher and how he had endeared himself to everyone he met.

Amid fresh spring flowers, Johanson's wife sang "I Am a Pilgrim" and "Someday We'll Understand" to the somber, overflowing assembly. One hundred cars were parked on Granite Street for what the *Boston Herald* described as the largest funeral in Rockport's history.[13]

Oker was buried at the Beech Grove Cemetery. August and Olof Olson, Herman Larson, Axel Andersen, Charles Johnson and Emil Ranta served as pallbearers. Detective Murray, Chief Sullivan and Officers Quinn and Allen attended the funeral and the interment. They carefully watched the mourners. Standing at the lip of the open grave, the reverend intoned prayers for the dead.

10

THE OKER INVESTIGATION

May 22–May 29, 1932

Chief Sullivan, Officer Quinn, State Detectives Murray and Griffin and ballistics expert W.H. Thompkins arrived at the crime scene at 77 Main Street on Sunday. Thompkins dusted the premises for prints, while an unnamed state police photographer took snaps. Newspapermen arrived in Rockport for a scoop.

The investigators discussed the case in between errands to interview witnesses. They were confounded. How did such a violent crime, one that smashed up a shop interior, occur without anybody hearing or seeing anything? It happened in a store on Main Street, along a row of cheek-by-jowl shops, on the busiest business shopping day of the week, within the fifteen minutes between a police officer looking in the shop window and the son unlocking the door. How did the killer batter Oker, grab his billfold, rifle the safe, switch vests, grab a topcoat, erase an appointment book entry and somehow sneak out unnoticed—all without anybody hearing or seeing anything?

Where was the murder weapon? His tailor shears were missing, yes, but the shears were probably not heavy enough to inflict the severity of wounds Oker received. So, if the shears weren't the weapon, what and where was it?

What about Oker? Did he have any enemies? Was he in financial trouble? Who was the straw-hatted man he talked to for so long? Were they putting together some sort of business deal? What about that lottery stub in the safe? The investigators heard a rumor that Oker had won a $1,100 lottery (the equivalent of $24,000 in 2024) the week prior. Was the straw hatted man a bookie? Was he a man who wanted a cut of Oker's winnings? Maybe it was a deal gone wrong—or a felony murder.

The Lottery Angle

Promoting a lottery or the possession of a lottery ticket was illegal in Massachusetts in 1932, having been banned for the past ninety-nine years. However, during the Depression, underground lotteries proliferated, with bookies hawking a variety of games. They sold out-of-state or even foreign country lottery tickets. There were a variety of nickel and dime numbers pools popular in New England (with a racist name no longer popular and never appropriate). There was the Treasury Balance, aka a Federal Reserve lottery, a numbers game in which the winning number was the same as the final number of the Federal Reserve bank balance, which was published in the dailies. The odds were terrible, but its randomness was government-backed, and a winning four-number combination could pay off a person's mortgage.

Numbers pools were typically played in poor or middle-class neighborhoods. In an era before the New Deal, it was often the only way a struggling family could get a windfall. Typically, the bets were placed at a semi-private location with a telephone, like a bar or shop. By 1932, the games were coming under the control of organized crime—and becoming known as "rackets."

It is not known what type of lottery ticket stub Oker had in his safe.

The only *Gloucester Daily Times* report of a numbers racket on Cape Ann immediately prior to the Oker murder was of the case of Henry Hendrickson, arrested by Gloucester police on April 1 for promoting a lottery and possessing lottery tickets. Hendrickson was discharged of both counts in district court and fined $100, but he was given a new charge of possession of out-of-state lottery tickets. He appealed and posted a $300 bail, likely paid by his underworld bosses.[14]

It is unknown if the lottery Hendrickson was running was the same game that Oker potentially participated in—if Oker participated in a lottery at all.

The Interviews

Police and detectives conducted a total of fifteen interviews of customers, shop owners and downtown residents. Police were looking for either a straw-hatted man or two sailors. Several witnesses claimed that they saw a man speeding through downtown in a tan coupe with a rumble seat, heading in the direction in Gloucester. None of them caught the license plate number.

Investigators followed up on Oker's morning phone call. Since Rockport was on the dial as opposed to the operator system, there was no way to trace it. The Ma Bell telephone company didn't keep records of calls.

Chief Sullivan and Detective Quinn traveled to Gloucester to interview two local men apprehended for failure to stop for police. The men were jumpy, suspected liquor smugglers. They were questioned and released.[15] They interrogated another suspect at the Gloucester Police Station, Rockport teenager Arve Willius, eighteen, arrested for drunkenness. The boy had a solid twenty-dollar bill in his pocket but a flimsy alibi about his windfall. Police determined he had stolen it from his father but cleared him of suspicion of murder.[16]

District Attorney Cregg arrived in Rockport to take charge of the investigation. He called Harvard University pathologist Dr. J. Stewart Rooney to come to Rockport that night to examine Oker's body. Cregg hoped Dr. Rooney could provide more information on the type of weapon used.

The investigators were stumped regarding the suspect and weapon. They were confident that robbery was the motive.

Monday, May 23, 1932

In the morning, Rockport Police went through their card catalog of local criminals, eager to establish their whereabouts and possible connection to the crime. Detectives Griffin and Murray and Chief Sullivan questioned a dozen witnesses at the police station, most of whom were at the tailor's shop the morning of the murder. They learned about the delivery of the package, which was missing from the crime scene. They asked the U.S. Postal Service to track it. They made phone calls, establishing Oker's financial forensics. State police fingerprint expert W.H. Thompkins and Captain Charles J. Van Ambergh visited Oker's shop to review the fingerprint evidence and look for other clues. The detectives did a walkthrough with Rudolph Oker at the crime scene. What did he see? What did he do? What did he do next?

Investigators were no longer confident that robbery was the motive.

Oker was an unlikely robbery victim. He was frugal, not flashy, a "quiet and courteous citizen," as his obituary reported. He was generous in extending credit to customers—a fact very well-appreciated in dark economic times. He had recently asked some of his customers who owed more than $100 to make a payment, but there were no reports of disagreements over the ask. He had sent some outstanding accounts to the Bay State Collection Agency, but the firm hadn't begun any collection work. Having interviewed the morning's customers, inspectors determined Oker had no more than $17 or $25 on hand. This did not include, of course, whatever was in the safe. But Oker didn't keep money in the safe. In fact, he never locked the safe. He always kept it in his billfold, which, admittedly, was missing.

Oker had a couple of side hustles. He had a large pressing business wherein he would iron people's clothes for a small fee. Regularly, perhaps weekly, he'd close the shop at noon, collect the payments and then go home for lunch. He also served as the local collection agent for the Gloucester Coal and Lumber Company, so occasionally, he did have sums of cash on hand. The *Gloucester Daily Times* reported that Oker had recently sold some old merchandise—at one point worth $1,000—to a man in Boston but didn't give the man who arranged the deal a commission. The man was reputedly angry and demanded Oker's phone number. But the investigators didn't think the man was murderously angry.[17]

The lottery angle washed out as well. There were no rumors of Oker running numbers or placing bets. The local gossip that Oker had won a lottery or recently gotten a big payout was a shock and complete surprise to his family. Arthur never told his family about any big winnings. As far as they knew, he never gambled.[18] The investigators checked the local banks. There was no record that Oker had made a large deposit in any of them.[19] The investigators checked their shady sources, questioning the man who sold the winning ticket, who in turn identified the lucky Rockport winner, who was not Oker.[20] The police interviewed three individuals who were known to sell pool and treasury balance lottery tickets on the North Shore. All three had alibis and were not near Rockport on the day of the murder. The man who was rumored to have sold the lottery ticket to Oker had not been seen in town since the attack.[21]

Investigators believed Oker knew the suspect. None of the witnesses recognized him. Maybe he was an out-of-towner. He was in the store at 10:30 a.m. and waited for Oker to finish business with two customers. The suspect knew the interior of the store and knew the view to the outside was obscured by clothing and other sale items in the display windows. Oker and the suspect had an involved conversation, one that required privacy. They surmised the attack was not premeditated but spontaneous. The killer struck the first blow and then followed Oker around the store, raining more blows on his head. Oker, attempting to protect his head with his hands, got his pinkies almost severed in the process. Oker collapsed behind the counter. The man—and the police were confident the assailant was a man—rifled Oker's pockets and took his wallet and keys, and he shuffled through the safe for valuables as a blind (i.e. a means to throw off authorities from the real motive). Then the murderer walked out the front door.

At this stage, police believed the missing tailor shears were the murder weapon, despite the pathologist's report stating that the wounds were more likely made by a hatchet. Per the orders of Chief Sullivan, Officer Zenas Conley spent three hours searching Front Beach and the back sides of buildings along Main Street for the shears from the east end of Back Harbor to the northwest end of the beach.

Newspaper journalists searched the Mill Pond area, specifically Back Beach and a vacant lot on King Street, on the theory that the killer fled the store and then made his way toward the Rockport Train Station to make the 1:00 p.m. train to Boston, tossing the murder weapon into the grass and rubbish that lined the route. The gentlemen of the press found nothing.

By the end of the day, state detectives had concluded their investigation of the crime scene and turned the premises back over to the Oker family.

Tuesday, May 24, 1932

Detectives Murray and Griffin arrived in Rockport in the morning and met up with Rockport Police officers. Together, they went around the town, checking up on initial statements and interviewing new witnesses. They learned nothing worthwhile by midday. Part of the issue was that Oker was well-respected, with no known scandals, peccadillos or enemies. But conversely, there were wild rumors of sexual harassment, affairs and sordid love triangles involving Arthur Oker or his married daughter Ellie with various paramours. These stories, generated by the febrile minds of gossipy Rockporters, got the basic facts of the murder case wrong. But the investigators gleaned that they were not getting the full story. In a statement to the press, the detectives and Chief Sullivan offered "full protection" to anyone who could provide information that could lead to the arrest of the killer. Chief Sullivan added, "I am sure there are several persons who are afraid to come forward with vital information because of their fear, either of the killer, or of the publicity that would result."[22]

The investigators were no longer confident the killer was an out-of-towner.

The *Gloucester Daily Times* reported that investigators were "baffled" and that the murder was not done by a professional. It continued:

> *Investigators do not believe there was any argument over any unpaid bill. They are certain, however, that something deeper was involved and are checking up on certain information which cannot be made public at this present time, to see if their hunch is correct.*[23]

The *Boston Post* reported:

> *Because of several peculiar circumstances, local angles of the probe will be exhausted before the authorities make any attempts to broadcast copies of the fingerprints.*[24]

That night, Rockport druggist Sydney Poole gave Officer James Quinn a pair of tailor shears, stating that Oker had lent them to him a year ago. Oker told Poole to hang on to them; if he needed them back, he'd ask. The shears did not match the description Mrs. Oker had given them, so the police planned to show her this pair to see if she recognized them.

Meanwhile, postal officials continued to track the whereabouts of the missing package. They were able to identify the sender and were checking up on the contents.[25]

Wednesday, May 25, 1932

State Detective Murray arrived in Rockport early in the morning and interviewed two people at length. Murray then went to Boston to check up on a clue he received in a phone call. He came back to Rockport to do another interview in the afternoon.

Marshall (aka Mansfield) Moulton, a Pigeon Cove resident and bus driver for the Gloucester Auto Bus Company, reported to state and Rockport Police that at 9:05 a.m. the previous Saturday, he saw a tall, "medium-complexioned" stranger wearing a brown topcoat and soft hat board the bus to Rockport at the bus stop in Gloucester. Moulton remembered the man because he asked for the fare price.[26]

Following up on their interview of Postman Wilson, investigators were still researching the possibility that two sailors were the attackers instead of the straw-hatted man. They asked the post office to follow up on the missing registered mail package. Newspapers reported that the package's wrapping and the canceled stamps were missing.

Investigators showed the tailor shears, turned in the previous night, to Mrs. Oker. She did not recognize them. These shears had black handles. She thought her husband's shears had red or bronze handles. The black-handled shears were eliminated as the possible murder weapon.

The Rockport Police asked all the local laundries and remaining tailors if any bloodstained clothing had been dropped off for cleaning. They asked the Gloucester Police to make the same inquiries to all tailors, laundromats and dry cleaners in America's oldest seaport. The police also ran a notice, "Appeal to Public in Seeking Slayer," in the *Boston Herald*.

Oker's will, drawn up years before by Attorney Sumner Y. Wheeler, was filed in probate court. Oker had left everything to his wife.

That night, a crowd gathered in Dock Square. There was a rumor that an arrest was imminent. The buzzing and excited crowd remained till midnight, then dispersed. There was no news, no arrest and no progress. Everyone left in the dark.

Thursday, May 26, 1932

On an unseasonably hot day, investigators arranged for witness Melvin Linder to attend a lineup of sailors at the U.S. Navy's Thatcher's Island Naval Radio Station. Chief radioman John M. Schmutz organized the event. It is unclear why investigators asked Linder to the lineup, as he was on team Mr. Straw Hat. Melvin Linder did not recognize any of the sailors.

Miss Lydia Salo on Granite Street told police that at 1:00 p.m. on the day of the murder, she saw a cream-colored coupe with a rumble seat up speed down Forest Street from King Street; it was going so fast, she wasn't sure it was going to make the turn. In the car was the straw-hatted man in his brown coat, one hand on the wheel and the other holding his hat firmly onto his head. Melvin Olson reported that he saw the cream-colored coupe and said the first three license plate numbers were "727," which was impossible because those high numbers had not yet been issued by the Registry of Motor Vehicles.[27] Edward Johnson of Forest Street claimed that he saw the car as well, taking the curve on two wheels, traveling an estimated fifty miles per hour. Another unnamed witness said that he saw the tan-colored coupe parked near the Oker store for most of Saturday morning. Police hinted that the automobile clue was corroborated by a member of the Oker family, presumably Rudolph.

The tan coupe turned down Railroad Avenue. If the coupe had turned right onto Main Street, it would have been heading toward Gloucester and off Cape Ann Island via the only vehicular exit point, "the cut," i.e. the Blynman Bridge choke point that separated downtown Gloucester from the Magnolia city section and the rest of Massachusetts. The problem was, however, that Gloucester Police weren't stationed at the bridge at noon on Saturdays. No authority saw the coupe leave the island—if it did leave the island.

DA Cregg contemplated asking Massachusetts Governor Joseph B. Ely to post a reward. Despite the lack of progress, the *Gloucester Daily Times* "Lookout" editorial crowed:

> *The value of cooperation between police and newspapermen was never more ably demonstrated than in the murder case at Rockport. Clues and valuable suggestions have been brought to light by the newspapermen, who have worked closely with nose to the ground, lending every assistance to State Officers William Murray and Richard Griffin of the district attorney's office to solve the crime. Long weary hours have the gentlemen of the press put into the work, and long after police have gone to bed. Barely taking time to snatch a bite of food, snatching their sleep when they could, the reporters went everywhere with the officers. It is a marked contrast in cooperation between the press and police in Rockport to that in other places. Both state officers have called the newspapermen in and their confidences have been respected. Chief of Police Sullivan, Officers Quinn, Spates, Conley and Allen all lent valuable assistance to the newspapers. One newspaperman covering the cases said that it was his 27th assignment on murder cases, and nowhere that he had been had he ever been given so much scope by the*

police who told the reporters to "do what they wanted to and go where they wanted to," Yes, indeed, it certainly is a very great pleasure to work with these gentlemen who represented the law.[28]

Friday, May 27, 1932

State police Lieutenant-Investigator Joseph Stokes arrived in Rockport to oversee the progress of the investigation. The reason he came to town was because there was no progress. The United States Postal Service was looking into the missing package. Detectives Murray and Griffin speculated that two men may have carried out the attack: one held Oker down while the other clubbed him. Or maybe it was a single attacker, not in a tan topcoat but some sort of khaki-colored uniform. Or perhaps there were two men in uniforms. The *Gloucester Daily Times* reported that the authorities had "practically nothing in their possession which at the present time is of any assistance to them in making an arrest" and that frustrated residents were contemplating setting up a reward for information that led to the apprehension and conviction of the killer.

Saturday, May 28, 1932

Two additional unnamed Massachusetts State Police investigators arrived in Rockport to assist in the case.

Rockport Police appealed for information in the *Gloucester Daily Times*, requesting that the customer who held the previous Saturday's 11:25 a.m. appointment with Oker to contact Chief Sullivan. Chief Sullivan assured the press that the person was not a suspect but that investigators believed Oker may have mentioned the name of his next—and final—visitor to the customer.

Police Appeal

Will the person who was at the store of Arthur F. Oker, 77 Main street, Rockport on Saturday, May 21, at 11.25 o'clock in the morning, being fitted to a suit of clothes, communicate in person, or by telegram, letter or telephone to

JOHN E. SULLIVAN
Chief of Police, Rockport, Mass.

From the Gloucester Daily Times/ *North of Boston Media Group.*

Rockport Police continued interviews throughout the day with individuals who might have known something—or anything. But the more interviews they did, the more apparent it became that no one knew anything.

But they did wrap up the case of the silver salesmen.

The Silver Salesmen
May 21–May 28, 1932

At 9:30 p.m. on May 26, police in Wrentham, on the border of Rhode Island, arrested two men on a moving violation. They were driving a dark blue coupe. It wasn't their coupe. The driver, Jerome B. McKenna of Springfield, Illinois, age twenty-eight, had an alibi. He claimed that he and his nondriving partner, T.M. Connolly of Providence, were silver salesmen, and they had borrowed the car from Essex resident Leroy Jensen back on May 21—the day of Oker's murder.

McKenna told the Wrentham Police, "Go ahead—call the fella whose car we borrowed." The police did and made inquiries with the car's owner, Jensen, who said something about letting a couple of guys borrow it.

Jensen then called the state police detectives in Rockport. The detectives contacted the Wrentham Police, who gave them the names of the duo. Jensen explained that at 1:00 p.m. the previous Saturday at the Depot Lunch, McKenna and his partner introduced themselves to the man as "salesmen of a silver concern" with a tale of woe. Their car had broken down. They needed a vehicle to make sales calls in Gloucester and Essex to potential clients, throwing in a few prominent names.

Silver-tongued McKenna got Jensen to loan them his car. There was no mention of money, at least in the papers. The alibi checked out but seemed off. Wrentham Police told McKenna and his buddy that they'd better head back to Rockport to clear their names, or they'd become persons of interest in a murder investigation.

The men drove back, past the police guard night shift at the Blynman Bridge, and headed through town, up Great Hill, down Broadway to the Rockport Police Station. Their arrival time was unrecorded, but it was probably in the early hours of May 27. Chief Sullivan grilled them and determined that the silver salesmen were innocent. However, he said they should go to town hall at 10:30 a.m. and check in with Detective Murray.

The silver salesmen didn't show up at town hall at 10:30 a.m. They didn't show up by midday. Perhaps the silver salesmen thought they were in the clear, having talked to Chief Sullivan. Perhaps Chief Sullivan didn't stress how imperative it was for them to talk to the state detectives.

They were not in the clear.

At 1:00 a.m. on May 28, Rockport Police traveled to a Gloucester hotel and placed Jerome McKenna in protective custody for the night. In the morning, the state detectives gave him a stern interview. But the silver salesmen were cleared of any involvement with the killing and cleared out. Presumably, Jensen got his car back.

11

THE DETECTIVES' DILEMMA

May 29–June 30, 1932

A little more than a week after Oker's murder, the combined investigative team of state and Rockport Police had made no progress. The victim had led a squeaky-clean life. The crime scene fingerprint evidence was useless. Witness statements were a contradictory tangle. They did not even have a definite suspect or suspects. They did not know a motive or at least have one they shared with the press. They had no murder weapon.

Tuesday, May 31, 1932

State police Detective Griffin traveled to Amesbury, where local police had just arrested a "William Williamson" and his companion "John Williamson" for peddling without a license.

William claimed to be twenty-one and from Cincinnati. John said he was from Lima, Ohio. Noticing that one of the men was dressed in a sailor's uniform, acting Amesbury Police Chief J. Fred Ives contacted the Essex County DA. Maybe that nautical outfit tied Williamson to the Oker murder.

Detective Griffin interviewed Williamson and his codefendant. Both men, presumably Depression "hobos," swore they had no knowledge of the murder. Griffin believed them. The two Williamsons were packed off to the Lawrence House of Correction.

Investigators traveled to Beverly to run down a tip—with no results. They interviewed three Rockport citizens, one for a second time.

Detectives held a conference with the Rockport Police and the DA at the station. They were now confident that the killer was a local. DA Cregg ordered Murray and Griffin to compile a list of names of all of Oker's known associates: business, social, religious and fraternal. Cregg asked that the list include people Oker had recently billed; perhaps he was killed by an irate customer.

Wednesday, June 1, 1932

State detectives were still in town, attempting to identify the tan coupe. They believed that Oker had known the killer well, but the killer was a stranger to Rockport.

Thursday, June 2, 1932

The investigation was on hold for the day while the entire Rockport Police Department traveled to Gloucester District Court to testify in a drunk driving case against Rockport popcorn merchant Russel Murch, who had driven his auto into a fish truck the previous Friday. Janitor Andrew Stevens remained behind to manage the station.

In their regularly scheduled evening meeting, the Rockport Selectmen voted to post a $500 reward to the person or persons who provided information that led to the arrest and conviction of the killer of Arthur F. Oker.[29]

Monday, June 13, 1932

Detective Murray submitted a status report on the Oker investigation to General Alfred Foot, commissioner of the Massachusetts State Police. The report gave a brief summary of the murder, the autopsy and the list of witnesses and persons interviewed. Murray described his effort to locate a "Carl Ericson [*sic*]," who was "formerly minister at Oker's church, and who was ousted, and Oker served on the board." Murray mentioned that he had heard a rumor that Ericson had left for Sweden on April 21.

In his report, Murray documented his correspondence with Chief Inspector John O'Brien of the New York Police Department. O'Brien, in turn, reported that there was no record of a "Carl David Erickson" leaving the port of New York, but there were three passengers with the name "Carl Erickson" aboard the Swedish American Line (SAL) ship *Drottningholm* that sailed for Sweden on April 21 and seven "Carl Ericksons" aboard the SAL liner *Gripsholm* that departed on May 28.[30]

Reverend David Erickson was a young, unmarried native of Sweden who had immigrated to the United States in 1923. In the fall of 1929, the SCC hired Reverend Erickson to replace the Reverend Waldemar Harrald, who was assuming the pastoral post at the Swedish Sailor's Home in East Boston. On September 12, 1929, the church held a welcoming ceremony for the new pastor, with Arthur Oker hosting as master of ceremonies. Reverend Erickson stayed with the Okers when he assumed his new role. The congregation welcomed its new Swedish-born pastor.

But for unknown reasons, Reverend Erickson did not work out.

A terse notice on the *Gloucester Daily Times* on June 2, 1931, stated, "David Erickson has closed his pastorage with the Swedish Congregational Church." The new pastor had lasted a year and a half. The paper did not report Erickson's future plans, as the Depression had deepened, and job openings had grown increasingly scarce. That edition did mention that Waldemar Harrald was visiting the Olson family in Rockport. Harrald was perhaps in town to act as a delicate negotiator and utility player as the SCC extricated itself from its current minister. As president and treasurer, the SCC's éminence grise, Oker would have presided over proceedings against the young minister and may have been the string-puller blamed for any drama. The SCC embarked on another search for a replacement, hiring Reverend Albert Johanson in October 1931.

Detective Murray apparently did not pursue the lead any further. Reverend Erickson's whereabouts between June 1931 and April or May 1932 are unknown. Of all persons of interest, Carl Erickson is easily the most chimerical. On the departure dates of the two Sweden-bound liners hinged opposite implications. The first provides an alibi, in effect confirming that Erickson was back in Sweden on the day of the murder.

The latter date suggests Erickson was a fugitive.

Tuesday, June 14, 1932

Chief Sullivan rounded up one of the usual suspects, arresting Daniel Chase of North Bergen, New Jersey. Chase was a former Rockport resident and career criminal with a rap sheet stretching back to 1913. This is his back story.

Bass Avenue resident Prescott Card reported that he'd been in his work shed on February 27 when he was approached by a man who was posing as a safety razor salesman. Despite Card's protestations, the insistent man entered the work shed, invaded Card's personal space and jostled him ("jounced up and down a couple of times") and then fled. It was then Card realized he'd been rolled of the $229 in his pocket. Card attempted to grab the man, but he got away. Card reported the theft, and on hearing a description of the man, Chief Sullivan had a hunch of who the man was, and he drew up a warrant for the arrest of Daniel Chase.

Then on June 14, Card recognized the man walking on Main Street. Card immediately went to the police station on Dock Square. The cops arrested Chase on the corner of Main and Pierce Streets for the outstanding warrant. His bail was set at an unreachable $1,000.

When Detective Murray heard of the arrest—strangely enough, not from Chief Sullivan—he headed over to the station. He and Chief Sullivan found a light felt hat, put it on Chase's head and brought in Melvin Linder and Postman Ralph Wilson separately to see if they could identify Chase as the man in Oker's shop. They could not. Chase had a similar build as that of the straw- (or felt-) hatted man, but his hair was lighter. He was no doubt a bad man, but he was not *their* man.

Thursday, June 30, 1932

A full week after the SCC's June 23 memorial service for Arthur Oker, state detectives stopped making regularly scheduled calls to the Rockport Police Station.

For over a month, the case preoccupied the Essex Country DA, an assistant DA, the state police lieutenant investigator, two state detectives, a photographer, a fingerprint expert, two doctors and the entire Rockport Police Department. Despite ten witnesses, thirty interviews, one lineup, two public appeals, two silver salesmen, reward money and forty days and forty nights, they could not solve who killed Arthur Oker.

The case was as cold as granite quarry rock.

12
INTERMISSION

June 1, 1932–October 30, 1933

The Oker family carried on despite the devastation they felt over the murder of their husband, father and grandfather. To settle Arthur's estate, the family ran advertisements in the June 3 and June 10 editions of the *Gloucester Daily Times*. Men's suits were on sale for a staggeringly low $9.95, while still-popular, durable Arrow collars were offered at two for a quarter. On June 11, the paper reported that young Rudolph Oker, along with Captain Roger Martin, planned to continue operating the family business at 77 Main Street.

On June 13, Rockport Police got a report of two men fighting on Back Beach. Chief Sullivan sent Officers Allan and Spates to investigate. On nearby Smith Street, they found Selectman Parker at the hand crank of his truck, which, in those days, was the key to ignite a vehicle's engine. Allan and Spates "deemed it best for the safety of the public to take him into custody" and arrested Parker for "wet driving." Parker posted the $200 bail and was ordered to appear in court on June 21.[31]

Six months later, the December 19 op-ed page of the *Gloucester Daily Times* published a letter from Selectman Parker:

Estate sale advertisement. *From the Gloucester Daily Times/North of Boston Media Group.*

To the editor of the Daily Times:

As chairman of the Board of Selectmen, it is my duty to call to the attention of the citizens any improper action of those appointed by the board as may be expedient for the benefit of the town. The residents of the town are calling for better police protection. It may as well be universally known that I have, for several years past, believed in a more efficient chief of police, and also believe that we should have a chief of police who would do his duty, regardless of political affiliation. The town government should be centered at Town hall, and nowhere else.

Does Mr. Sullivan do his duty? I will cite a few of the many cases that may be considered....The Oker murder case: The discovery of Mr. Oker's assault occurred about 12:30 p.m. on Saturday. The police were notified and went to the premises. Instead of locking the door and keeping out the curious public, they were allowed to come in and destroy all tangible evidence. As far as we know, there are no strong clues at present.[32]

Even prior to the June drunk driving arrest, Parker and Chief Sullivan had been at odds. Sullivan favored a 1929 proposed legislature bill that would have not only provided the chief with civil service benefits without a fitness test but also stripped the selectmen of reappointment power; Parker traveled to the state house to testify against it. Parker described himself as "the first man to be able to hold an office on the board of selectmen, when Mr. Sullivan was opposed to that action" and mentioned his April 1932 vote against Sullivan's reappointment.

In his op-ed letter, Selectman Parker claimed that Chief Sullivan had failed to protect the Oker crime scene, thus jeopardizing the investigation from the start. Allowing members of the public to wander into Oker's store on May 21, possibly moving, removing or otherwise contaminating evidence, was a bombshell of an accusation, calling into question Sullivan's competency not just as chief but also as a law enforcement officer.

The Swedish Congregational Church also carried on despite the tragic loss of its president. On December 20, the twenty-five-voice SCC choir, paired with the Swedish Glee Club of Rockport, gave its annual Christmas concert, singing Swedish hymns such as "Christmas Is Here," "When Christmas Morn Is Breaking" and "Hark, Hark My Soul." On January 5, 1933, the SCC held its fortieth annual meeting. Reverend Johanson gave the sermon in Swedish, citing Isaiah 61:2, "Preach for a year of the grace of the Lord." He continued:

The year of 1932 now ended in the books, but a new year of grace, 1933, has begun. It is good for us to remember both that which we are happy about and what is humiliating....Many things have been written that we now wish were not....But we have an option: this is to admit, regret, and improve—this leads to the chair of grace where all will be forgiven, and our list of guilt erased. God's grace should not cause us to be careless, but learn to act more wisely in the future.[33]

The congregation then voted August Olson, its former Sunday school superintendent, to be church president. Mrs. Oker remained involved as a deaconess and member of the Ladies Aid Society. She hosted a gathering of the society on March 14 at her home on Main Street to discuss its mission of "scattering sunshine and lifting burdens" to the aged, infirm and ill with cards, visits and flowers.

At the end of 1932, the SCC wrote a history of the church. Reverend Johanson was likely the author of the document. This short, seven-page document had this to say about the church's former president:

It is with sadness and grief that I have to convey the message to you that Mr. Arthur P. Oker, born on December 7, 1874 in Nurmijarvi, Finland has passed away while being the victim of a murderer on Saturday, May 21, 1932....[His children] stand with their mother and their families struck by the deepest grief and pain. This entire community participates in their grief. The congregation in which he was a real pillar of strength as their chairman the past few years, joins in the grief. He left a great void both at home and in this church and in the community. Few have been so loved and cherished in this community as our friend Oker. Therefore, we are all struck and taken aback that he would end his days in this way.

But such events, although horrendous, are not entirely unusual. Several of the best presidents of this country have become victims of cruel murderers. But his peaceful little community of Rockport, where there has never been a similar crime before, is stunned with pain and grief. Our dear friend Oker was prepared to leave us; he died in the trust in his Redeemer, but we could not understand why he, right now, would leave us in this way.[34]

In March 1933, all the Rockport Selectmen were re-elected, though Chairman Ralph Parker barely squeaked by as the tail-end charlie with the least number of votes.

District Attorney Hugh Cregg had his hands full with the Costello trial. Jessie Burnett Costello of Peabody was charged with murder, accused of poisoning her Irish firefighter husband with cyanide. She had reputedly been having an affair with their roommate, a Peabody policeman. This rumored love triangle lured spectators to her trial, along with a bevy of reporters. Cregg was no match for Costello—she was well-figured, well-spoken and, well, acquitted. Although Cregg got points for solid trial oratory, his failure to convict was considered egg on his face.

By the fall of 1933, Rockport had a church mulling over guilt and forgiveness, town officials at each other's throats, allegations of a botched investigation and a DA eager to recoup his reputation.

Given future events, that scenario would not bode well.

13

ADA JOHNSON, MODEL CITIZEN

Auburn-haired Augusta "Ada" Palson, age fifty-five, was born in Sweden. She arrived in the United States in 1900, where she found work as a domestic in Boston and Brookline. A stout but attractive woman, Ada married a Rockport widower, the stonecutter Adolph Johnson, in April 1921. She quit being a domestic and moved into his tidy home with a wraparound porch on 1 Oakland Avenue, just off Pigeon Hill Street.

Adolph Johnson, a taciturn member of the Spiran Lodge who was well respected in Rockport's Swedish community, had a green thumb and an eye for thrift. On a workingman's wages, Johnson had saved enough to purchase multiple rental properties—a "corporation house" on Broadway, an apartment house on Curtis Street, an orchard and possibly one building in Gloucester. From the orchard, Adolph grew Baldwin apples and sold them out of his house, which was surrounded by beds of flowers that he carefully tended.

When Reverend Waldemar Harrald, the SCC's previous pastor, arrived in Rockport from Brattleboro, Vermont, in 1924, Adolph and Ada put him up at their home. Harrald enjoyed his stay and later described the Johnsons as a lovely couple. Although they were involved in several societies, neither belonged to the SCC. Harrald invited the Johnsons to join the church on multiple occasions, but they politely declined, although they would attend services on Christmas and Easter and the occasional church social.

By 1930, Adolph was ill with "stonecutter's TB" (silicosis) and could no longer work. He died ten days after the Oker murder, on Memorial Day 1932, at his home on Oakland Avenue, which became the site of his funeral. He and Ada had had no children, but he left several surviving relatives: a brother in Denmark; another brother and sister in Sweden; a brother, Oscar Johnson, in New Bedford; and a sister, Mrs. Anna Stolpe; and his mother, Albertina, in Rockport.

By Adolph's will, the bulk of the estate went to Ada, including the multiple properties, valued at $5,000. However, the granite monument (for $1,000) and several legacy bequests whittled cash assets of the estate that Ada inherited down to $875. The couple's next-door neighbor, August Olson, served as the trusted executor; Sumner Y. Wheeler of 17 Pleasant Street served as the estate attorney.

Ada Johnson. *From the* Boston American.

Ada carried on after her husband's death. She kept the house immaculate and grew vegetables and beautiful flowers in her yard. She raised chickens and sold the eggs to neighbors. She kept a canary as a pet. She attended services at the SCC more regularly and took part in its social activities, although she was still not a pledged member. She was solid in multiple senses of the word—stocky at 160 pounds—and held in high esteem by her neighbors in Pigeon Hill's largely Swedish community.

Although her closest blood relatives were her siblings in Illinois, Ada kept in closer contact with her husband's family. Through marriage, Ada had two nieces and a nephew in Lynn, Mrs. Esther Coggin, Mrs. Ardell J. Delaney and Carl Stolpe, and another niece, Mrs. Nannie Erickson, in Boston. Every Wednesday morning, Ada and her sister-in-law Anna would walk to Beech Grove Cemetery on Pleasant Street to leave flowers on Adolph's grave.

On October 17, 1933, Ada paid $120 in property taxes, probably in cash, at town hall. She was financially comfortable with her rental properties, but still, as a relatively young widow, she needed to live frugally. She collected rents in person at the end of each month.

On October 24, Ada visited the Ericksons on Commonwealth Avenue in Boston to celebrate the birthday of their children Lillian and Leonard. The twins had turned six. She spent the afternoon with them and then took a train back to Rockport. During her visit, Ada mentioned nothing unusual or of note. She was never one to be reticent. If she seemed fine, she was fine. Reverend Harrald later commented, "She was a quiet woman of the independent type. She would fight for her rights; she would fight for what she thought right. She was a strong woman."[35]

14

THE HALLOWEEN PARTY

Tuesday Evening, October 31, 1933

The SCC held a combined surprise party and harvest social for Pastor Albert Johanson at his home at 177 Main Street to celebrate his second anniversary with the congregation. It was two days before the full moon.

The party was fun. Anywhere from nine to twenty people attended; although given the events to come, recollections and alibis got a little fuzzy. Verified attendees included the following:

- Pastor Albert Johanson
- Mrs. Albert Johanson, the pastor's wife
- Ada Johnson
- Albertina Johnson, Ada Johnson's mother-in-law
- Hilda (Mrs. August) Anderson
- Mrs. John J. Lundgren
- August Olson
- Warren Olson
- Olof Olson, August Olson's brother
- Agusta Olson, Olof's wife
- Anna Stolpe, Ada Johnson's sister-in-law
- A visiting Bible-selling minister from Brooklyn, New York, probably a former colleague of Pastor Johanson

Partygoers later described Ada at the party as "jolly" and in "the best of health." She showed some guests her diamond solitaire ring in a Tiffany prong setting style that was popular before World War I, worn next to her wedding band on the ring finger of her left hand. She briefly spoke to the salesman, promising to buy a Bible the next day.

The party broke up around 10:20 p.m. Albertina Johnson was planning to stay the night with Ada, but at the last minute, she decided to go back to her house. The Bible salesman was spending the night with Carl Strandhal, the church caretaker. August Olson offered to drive people home in his car.

What happened next is a little unclear.

Adolph, Warren, Olof and Agusta got into the car. Ada Johnson got into the car. Hilda Anderson got into the car. Mrs. Lundgren got into the car. It must have been a big car to fit seven people. The sequence of drop-offs was likely but not certainly: Olof and Agusta, Hilda, Mrs. Lungren and, finally, Ada.[36]

At around 10:30 p.m., August Olson let Ada out of the car at her home on Oakland Avenue. August told Warren to take the car back to the minister's house and to get anyone else who needed a ride home. The *Boston Herald* did not mention that he asked Warren to go back to the pastor's house. August walked Ada to her door. He asked her if she wanted "the men folks to enter the house first to see if everything was all right."

She replied no, she wasn't afraid of being alone.

He may have seen her go into the house and turn on the light.

August Olson may have gone back to Ada's house. The *Boston American* reported that August said he visited for fifteen minutes, talking about the party. The *Boston Herald* reported that he stayed for fifteen minutes and that she "let her hair down." He claimed that he was back home around 10:45 p.m. His wife did not know he had spent fifteen minutes with Ada until later the next day.[37]

Warren arrived home at 11:00 p.m. His parents were presumably asleep in their bedroom upstairs. He settled himself into the kitchen. He had work to do, painting lettering on signs for an upcoming Ladies' Aid Society performance and fundraiser the following Wednesday. He got his brushes and paints out and began to carefully fill the stems, strokes and shoulders of the lettering.

15

THE PYRE

Wednesday, November 1, 1933

6:00–8:45 a.m.

At 6:00 a.m. the next morning—Wednesday, All Souls Day—August Olson left his house. Oakland Avenue was a quiet, narrow lane near Curtis Street, one of Rockport's main roads. Broad-shouldered August was off to pick up several other carpoolers and drive to work in Lynn. As he got into the driver's seat, he glanced over at Ada's house, which was just thirty feet away. In the autumn dawn, he noticed nothing amiss.

At 8:20 a.m., William Carne of Pigeon Hill Street, the stonecutter father of SCC organist Blanche Carne, was walking down Oakland Avenue when he noticed thick, black smoke oozing out of the edges of a closed upstairs window on the northern side of Ada Johnson's house. Rushing to her front door, he shouted and pounded, but the door was locked, and he heard no answer from inside. Carne ran across the street to the Olson house. Warren Olson, in his slippers, answered the door.

"There's a fire!" Carne shouted.

From there, recollections—or at least newspaper reports—conflict.

Carne ran down the street and pulled the fire alarm at Fire Box no. 63. Or Olson may have pulled the lever on the box.

Warren Olson ran to Ada's house. The front door was locked. He ran to the back of the house.

The back door was locked, but the adjacent back pantry window was unlatched. He crawled through the window. He saw no smoke or fire downstairs nor smoke coming from the cellar. He ran up the stairs to the second floor. The smoke was worse up there. He strode down the hallway toward the bedroom. He entered the bedroom, where the smoke was thickest. Ada Johnson was on the bed. The bed was on fire.

The fire's searing heat and toxic smoke made it difficult to breathe. Warren turned to the adjacent upstairs bathroom and quickly ran water under a towel. He wrapped a towel around his head to protect himself from the heat and the smoke. He may have used the towel to beat back the flames; he might have pressed the towel on Ada's face to help her. Any attempt to put out the blaze was fruitless.

Warren may have retreated from the bedroom. He may have opened a side door to let Carne in. Warren may have crawled out of the pantry window. It is unclear why he did not use the door.

A passerby named Otto Erickson arrived on the scene as the fire department's chemical and pump engine pulled up. Warren, Carne, Erickson and the firemen may have briefly conferred together outside the house. At this point, the doors to the house may have been unlocked.

Fire Chief Levi Thurston ran a ladder up the side of the wraparound porch. Standing on the porch roof, fireman John Sherburne smashed the bedroom window's glass, climbed through and ran a hose into the bedroom. Other firemen, by this time, may have gained access to the home via a door. They tramped up the stairs through the hallway, where the smoke was still thick. The firemen used chemical fire retardant. The fire was confined to the bedroom. The firemen threw half a burning mattress out the broken window and onto the front lawn, where it smoldered. The firemen extinguished the fire in the bedroom.

Chief Sullivan arrived and went upstairs. The first responders crowded around Ada Johnson, who was lying in the burnt remnants of her bed. Ada Johnson could not be saved, for she was dead.

16

TORCH SLAYER

The Johnson Murder

WEDNESDAY, NOVEMBER 1, 1933

8:45 A.M.–11:00 P.M.

At 8:45 a.m., Anna Stolpe arrived at Ada's house to for their weekly visit to Adolph's grave. After seeing the fire and policemen and hearing the news, Anna collapsed. Onlookers took her to a neighbor's house.

At 9:20 a.m., Ada's physician, Dr. Cleaves, arrived. He entered the bedroom. He refused to say anything definite until someone from the district attorney's office came. Glancing at the corpse, he knew this death was suspicious.

Chief Sullivan called District Attorney Cregg, who, in turn, dispatched Assistant DA Charles, Detectives Griffin and Murray and fingerprint expert Sergeant Toelken immediately to 1 Oakland Avenue. The DA would arrive later. The state detectives entered the house and headed for the bedroom.

The bedding and mattress were badly burned and now partially destroyed, with half of it thrown onto the front lawn. Ada lay on the pyre partially naked in the ashen remnants of a kimono, her arms placed over her head. The position of her arms led to erroneous news reports that she had been tied down. Ada's left hand and forearm were burned off to the elbow. Her left leg was badly charred; some accounts state her left foot was burnt off. Her breasts were burnt. Ada's right arm, face and right leg were undamaged, probably due to being covered with bedding or pillows. The heat and smoke had blackened and damaged her wire-rimmed bifocals. But it was her head, on which those bifocals rested, that was most gruesome.

Gently moving Ada's body, the investigators saw a massive skull fracture from the top of her head to her left ear and a gaping V-shaped hole several inches wide on the back of her skull, with her brain exposed, bruised and torn. Around the wound were another half-dozen scalp wounds, as if made by a heavy blunt instrument, perhaps a stonemason's hand brush or ball-peen hammer.

Sergeant Toelken got out his camera and fingerprint kit. He began the preliminary investigation of a messy crime scene, toxic with the smell of rancid chemicals and charred flesh.

The bedroom lamp was lit when the firemen entered. Ada must have switched it on during the night. Sunrise that day was at 6:20 a.m. Dawn was probably around 5:50 a.m. The *Gloucester Daily Times* would later write that Ada's clean housekeeping was "a trait of her people": "Her clothes were laid out on the chair in her bedroom with a neatness and precision that showed the methodical type she was." The investigators found a strongbox in the bedroom closet with a key in the lock and financial papers inside. On the bedside table was a fire-damaged Fashion alarm clock with the time stopped at 5:48.

Upstairs, there was Ada's bedroom, another bedroom, a bathroom and the hallway. When the firemen first arrived, the smoke was so thick in the hall that they could barely see and weren't sure what they had slipped on. With the smoke dissipated, the investigators saw the blood splatters on the wall, the trail of bloody footprints and a huge puddle of blood on the threshold of the adjacent bedroom. There was a bloody clump on the floor below one of the smears on the wall.

It was a lump of skin and hair attached to a bone shard.

The dining room downstairs looked untouched, with a silver set on the sideboard. On the dining table was a pocketbook with five dollars inside. The investigators made a note to dust it for fingerprints.

In the pantry, Griffin, Murray and Sullivan saw two broken items on the floor, a bottle of polish and a small china pitcher. They appeared to have fallen when someone attempted to crawl in the pantry window. There was a bread container or flour tin on the shelf below the window. On it was a blood smear. There was another blood smear on the inside of the sill. There was a slight hole in the glass pane on the right side of the central wooden support, facing in, where the sash lock was.

There was no murder weapon found on the premises.

Outside on the south side of the property, near the side of the house, lay a blue Milk of Magnesia bottle. Nearby on the lawn lay a lady's black pocketbook containing six cents and a paid electric bill. There were muddy footprints outside the pantry window, which led from the house, across a garden in the rear of the house and toward a back road. In the roadway, police found auto tire tracks. Was this a critical clue or just random tracks on a muddy road?

A crowd of onlookers at the crime scene. *From the* Boston American.

Gawkers were everywhere outside. The crowd had gotten so large that they trampled the flower beds, originally planted by Mr. Johnson, and the vegetable garden. One neighbor, surveying the scene, remarked, "Old Johnson would turn over in his grave if he could see the way those morbid crowds were trampling his flowers." Chief Sullivan ordered Officers Zenas Conley and Spates to guard the residence to keep out anyone not there on official business.

Perhaps to cut down on the crowds surrounding the house, Chief Sullivan, the habitual old organizer, formed a civilian search party to hunt for clues. Twenty-five young men and teenagers canvassed the Pigeon Hill neighborhood. They quickly returned with bloody newspapers.

At midday, District Attorney Cregg arrived. At some point in the afternoon, the remnants of the burnt mattress on the front lawn were dragged to the back lawn. At 4:30 p.m., local undertaker Elmer Burgess took Ada's body to Addison Gilbert Hospital for an autopsy.

Cregg and investigators left the crime scene and went to the Rockport Police Station for a conference and to make phone calls. Chief Sullivan called the police in Gloucester and surrounding towns, asking them to be on the lookout for a man wearing bloodstained clothes in an automobile. The DA called General Needham, commander of the Massachusetts State Police, requesting the release of state troopers to assist in the investigation. General Needham agreed to release eight state troopers, several of whom would be dispatched to Rockport immediately from the Topsfield State Barracks.

The investigators reviewed the facts. Ada was a Swedish immigrant widow who attended a church party the previous night. Given the victim's head wounds, her death appeared to be the result of a homicide, committed during a robbery. It was the first of the month; Ada was a landlord and probably had cash on hand from her rentals, so her attacker was probably a desperate local man who killed her for her money. Or, given the proximity of her house to the woods, wild areas and abandoned quarries of Rockport, perhaps a Depression "hobo" killed her. The vagabond might still be hiding.

Then another member of the same church who met an unnatural end seventeen months previously sprang to mind.

A positive development was that there appeared to be a lot of fingerprints on the crime scene. Given the amount of evidence, this case could be solved quickly.

Meanwhile, the Rockport Selectmen met at town hall in an emergency session. They voted to offer a $1,000 reward for any information that led to the apprehension and conviction of the killer. The selectmen adjourned and then walked down the street to the police station to meet with the investigators. Selectman Roy Lane notified the investigators about the selectmen's reward. The selectmen then asked the DA if Essex County could put up another $1,000 in reward money. The DA said he would investigate. They asked Cregg to spare no expense in finding the murderer. Cregg told the selectmen and Chief Sullivan that he would solve this case even if he had to interview every single Rockport resident and bring in every police officer in Massachusetts.

The group then walked back to town hall for another conference and to take witness statements. The selectmen offered their office as a place for the DA to conduct witness questioning. Cregg accepted the offer.

At this point, the investigation team included DA Cregg, Chief Sullivan, State Detectives Murray and Griffin, Rockport Officer James Quinn and State Troopers William Faron and Francis Byrne from Topsfield. Salem Police Sergeant Thomas F. Hyde, who was officially on vacation but in town visiting his in-laws, offered to help.

There was some sort of press conference. State police detectives confidently told the newspapers that they expected to make a swift arrest, given the fingerprint and footprint evidence. They had men on the scene and elsewhere, gathering evidence and conducting interviews. The press asked questions about the similarities and possible connections between the Ada Johnson death and the Arthur Oker murder. The investigators conceded that the cases might be linked.

Late-edition newspapers would report on how splendidly the investigation was progressing and how diligently collaborative the DA's office, the Rockport Police, the state police and the press were. With the headline "Chief Sullivan on Job," the *Gloucester Daily Times* wrote, "Police Chief John E. Sullivan deserved much credit for the able manner in which he handled the case up to the time of the district attorney's appearance in the forenoon."

The papers would also report that the Pigeon Cove neighborhood was terrified by the recent news. The *Gloucester Daily Times* reported that the attack was the work of a "maniac."

The witness statement sessions began.

Cregg's first witness was August Olson, who recounted dropping off Ada at her house the night before the murder. He said that she entered the house alone. Olson mentioned, "She always had money in the bank and when she needed it she drew it out. She often spoke of having to scrape up money for incidental expenses and I really do not believe there was more than the five dollars found at her house at the time of her murder."

August Olson. *From the Boston Post.*

Cregg next interviewed Warren Olson, who had discovered the body.

Friend of the deceased Mrs. Sigrid A. Johnson of 11 Story Street gave a statement, as did Anna Stolpe and Hilda Anderson. William R. Mackay of 41 Pigeon Hill Street reported that he saw a suspicious person in the neighborhood when he went to work that morning. Investigators questioned Jalmer Kouveas of Stockholm Avenue, whom the detectives thought might know something pertinent. A previous American Legion Post commander, Francis A. McDonald, gave a statement. Lewis Patriquin, a counterman at the Hesperus Lunch Cart on Main Street in Gloucester, reported seeing a suspicious person at 2:00 a.m. Halloween night. Howard Gouin backed up Patriquin's statement. That lead was quickly eliminated.

Jeweler Joseph W. Thibeault confirmed that Ada's alarm clock would have stopped when the heat snapped the springs in the mechanism. He guessed that the clock was last wound at 11:00 p.m., probably when Ada went to bed.

Cregg questioned Ada's attorney, Summer Wheeler, at length about Adolph Johnson's will and if there was any family infighting over the estate.

The DA and his investigators conducted interviews until 11:00 p.m. and then headed over to the home of the pastor of the SCC.

17

THE MIDNIGHT MASS

Wednesday, November 1–Thursday, November 2, 1933

11:00 p.m.–2:00 a.m.

In the late evening, the DA went to the Johanson house and asked the reverend for a list of all the members of the SCC. The reverend supplied the list. At 11:00 p.m., State Troopers Faron and Byrne went door to door in the Pigeon Cove and Pigeon Hill neighborhoods, rousing the members out of bed and ordering them to assemble at the church.

The night was cold and clear. Compliant parishioners put on their coats and hats, walked or drove to church and sat silently in the pews. All the members were gathered by 1:00 a.m. Revered Johanson was sitting not up front but with his flock. Gathered in the back were journalists from multiple newspapers.

At the pulpit stood District Attorney Cregg, facing the congregation. He was flanked by State Detectives Griffin and Murray. Next to each detective stood a uniformed and armed state police trooper.

The DA, an experienced campaigner and savvy public speaker, began, "You are all members of this community. We need the help of all of you in locating this murderer now at large. There have been two brutal murders by a fiend."

The DA mentioned a couple clues to the members. He said that the investigators didn't believe robbery was the motive. He mentioned the similarity of Ada's case to the Oker murder last year.

Everyone stared at the DA, expressionless. Nobody spoke or stirred. Cregg continued,

> *I want every one of you to turn detective, not only to bring the murderer to justice, but to protect your own lives. I want you to think back upon anything unusual that might have happened—that you might have forgotten. Think back carefully. You gave a surprise Halloween party for your pastor, Reverend Albert Johanson. You were there. She went home from there to be brutally killed. I want you to think back.*
>
> *There have been two members of your congregation brutally murdered in the past year and a half. Perhaps the slayer of Mrs. Johnson and Arthur Oker is among you here. As far as you or I know, he may be here right now.*
>
> *Every one of you is under suspicion. I want to warn you that there is a killer in your midst and you—and you—and you—may be the next victim.*

With each *you*, the DA pointed to a different person in a pew.

"I am asking every one of you to be vigilant and co-operate with the authorities to bring about the apprehension of this fiend. Help me on this. That is all then. Keep thinking—or you may be next."

There was a stunned silence. An unnamed member of the congregation broke it by shouting that everyone assembled should be fingerprinted.

The DA replied that wouldn't be necessary—at this time.

A congregant made a motion for the assembled to give all assistance to the investigation. The motion passed.

Boston Globe journalist Geoffrey Parsons Jr. wrote, "As he spoke these words, there was a tenseness in the air that was entirely foreign to this place of worship." *Boston American* journalist James J. Smith described the event as "eerie" and speculated that this midnight mass was a psychological stress test to check the reactions of the sixty congregants.

The DA dismissed the SCC. The congregation broke into little groups and headed home under the moonlight along the dark shore.

18

THE JOHNSON INVESTIGATION

Thursday, November 2, 1933

Rockport was terrified, its new theme "distrust thy neighbor." Everyone, especially in Rockport's Swedish and Finnish communities, was under suspicion. The *Boston American* described Ada's murder as the "perfect crime." Both the populace and the press immediately connected Ada's death to the Oker case. The *Boston Globe* pointed out that both murder victims were Swedes, both were relatively well-off, both expected to collect their rents around the time that they were murdered; the paper stated, "Now comes the inevitable conclusion that someone thoroughly familiar with the habits of these retiring and close-mouthed people might have done these deeds. Perhaps the same person."

The district attorney personally took charge, with Detective Griffin running the daily operations. The Rockport Selectmen gave District Attorney Cregg use of their office. They placed a temporary sign on the door, reading, "Public Welfare," for as the *Gloucester Daily Times* reported, "There is nothing more important for the public welfare than the apprehension of the slayer." They set up camp beds in one of the anterooms for detectives to catch a nap.

Gloucester police patrolled the Blynman Bridge, guarding the single road in or out of Cape Ann. When the bridge was up, Gloucester and Rockport were cut off, separated from the mainland by a moat called the Annisquam River. Police now guarded the windswept single road in or out of Cape Ann like a border, checking vehicles and stopping anyone deemed suspicious.

At the police station, residents swarmed Chief Sullivan with requests for concealed carry firearms permits.

Officer Spates, who had been guarding Ada's house nonstop, asked one of her neighbors to take care of her hens. The luckless cluckers had run out of feed. Selectman Roy Lane wandered around the backyard, looking for bloodstains on fallen leaves.

Police checked the stone wall that bordered the Johnson property and the woodlot. No bloodstains were on the rocks. Perhaps the killer did not hop the wall to make his escape.

State detectives and policemen went door to door to all the houses within a half mile of Ada's house. They asked each neighbor if they were out or heard anything between 4:00 a.m. and 8:20 a.m. the day before.

Some neighbors were flagged for further questioning, including a muscular Finn who had great skill with quarry tools and who owned a small quarry, or "motion," one hundred feet from Ada's house. He was questioned three times, once for four hours, before he was cleared. Then eight state troopers from the Topsfield Barracks dragged his motion, looking for a discarded murder weapon. The quarry was deep; the task was futile.

The Rockport Selectmen met again in a special session. Chairman Parker phoned Robert H. Mitchell, chairman of the Essex County Commissioners, to ask if the county could pony up another $1,000 in reward money. Mitchell said he would bring up the matter at a special board meeting later that day and asked that Parker follow up with a written request. Mitchell told the *Boston Post*:

> *It is a particularly brutal crime. All the encouragement possible should be given in this case, so that the authorities can reach a solution of the mystery. I understand that other county governments have appropriated money for rewards in like situations, but I am not certain whether it is legal or not.... Within my knowledge, it has never been done in Essex County.*[38]

The selectmen discussed petitioning the governor for additional reward monies. Board chair Ralph Parker admitted to a *Globe* reporter that he hoped to win the $1,000 reward. He said that the selectmen all had the right to compete for it, just like any other town citizen.

Chief Sullivan requested that the selectmen hire two Gloucester policemen to augment the Rockport Police force. The Rockport Selectmen got in touch with Gloucester. City Marshal Daniel Casey loaned Special Officers J. Russell Moody and J. Henry Burgess to Rockport and instructed the Gloucester Police

Department to provide any assistance possible to the DA's investigation. The Rockport town clerk swore Burgess and Moody in as special officers.

A visibly distraught woman came to town hall. She claimed that her estranged husband was living in a shack in the woods. She thought that he might know something about the crime.

Detective Griffin, Assistant DA Green and State Fire Inspector James Trainor inspected the fire damage at Ada Johnson's house, which had been contained to one room on the second floor.

Twenty-five people, several of them members of the SCC, had come to the police station to form a volunteer search party. By 1:00 p.m., scores of people were milling around the Johnson house. Some were eager to help, encouraged by the selectmen. Some were eager for the reward money. Some were gawkers. Alvin Brown's legendarily public-spirited Boy Scout troop arrived, as did two dozen Rockport High School students after class. The crowds further trampled Ada's vegetable and flower gardens. DA Cregg gave the assembled citizens a brief introduction to criminology and sent them off to search the woods and fields near the murder scene for a weapon or bloody clothing. A group of children, some as young as five years old, surrounded the police sketch artist who was drawing a picture of Ada Johnson's house.

Detectives then interviewed fifteen people at town hall. Sigrid Johnson and August Olson were asked about what they saw when they left for work at 6:00 a.m. No, they did not hear or smell anything. Warren Olson was questioned again. Oscar Johnson, Ada's brother-in-law, provided useful information about Ada's finances. Mrs. Stolpe was questioned. She told a strange story about getting a phone call at 8:30 a.m. the morning of the murder, just before heading over to Ada's. She did not recognize the voice on the line. The unidentified caller asked if Mrs. Johnson was at home. It's unknown how Mrs. Stolpe replied, though "she was surprised at the inquiry, but thought no more about it."

The DA wanted to talk to a young woman who had solicited Ada a week before for a magazine subscription. The young saleswoman apparently spoke to a neighbor about Ada as a sales prospect and displayed an unusual interest in her finances. Cregg wondered if the girl could have been an accomplice.

The DA conducted a reenactment of Johanson's surprise party, which the *Boston Daily Record* described as "weird, "spooky" and "macabre." Cregg gathered all the attendees of the Halloween party together and went over exactly what they said and did—and what Ada said and did. The Bible salesman was presumably not present.

Financial Forensics

Ada Johnson was not poor, nor struggling, but contrary to press reports, she was not a wealthy widow. Her bank accounts contained $3,784.80 and $1,730.74 in the Cape Ann Savings Bank and $2,054.06 in the Rockport Granite Savings Bank. She took out $50 from one account on October 4 and $50 from the other account on October 13. She lived frugally, withdrawing small amounts from her savings accounts when she needed them.

The investigators learned through interviews that Ada did not keep large sums of money in her house. She had even previously expressed relief that she was able to "scratch together" her $120 property tax bill.

She had $4,600 in property value and was a landlady. Not all her units were rented out. Rents were due on the first of each month. She would go to collect them on or after that day. The total sum of the rents was roughly $50 (about $1,000 in 2024). Upon her death, she had not yet collected the November rent.

The investigators went through the strongbox or safety deposit box found in her room. Newspaper reports differed on whether the box was found in her closet or on her dresser, but all accounts agreed that the box was unmolested, with the key still in the lock. The box contained bank books, some canceled mortgages and a giveaway notebook Ada had received from a Gloucester insurance salesman. Folded inside the notebook was a letter and a newspaper clipping. The newspaper clipping was about a Gloucester man who was arrested for larceny roughly six months prior—though larceny was perhaps too strong a term for the crime given the context of the Depression. The man had gotten in trouble for being short on his accounts. The letter itself was from that man.

Ada had no life insurance; she once had a policy but had allowed it to lapse. Investigators suspected that her decision not to renew her policy may have had some bearing on the letter and the newspaper clipping. The detectives were eager to talk to that man, whose name they would not release to newspapers.

Per the investigators' conversation with Attorney Sumner Wheeler, Ada had no will. August Olson was the executor of Ada's husband's estate, but there were no reports of any contentious proceedings. Some of the Johnson's relatives, such as Esther Coggin, inherited relatively small bequests from Johnson's will—in this case $500—but again, there was no known dissension concerning the settlement of Johnson's affairs.

As for personal relations, all of Ada's neighbors, relatives, friends and acquaintances reported that Ada was a kind woman, well-liked by all. Ada's niece Dorothy Hammond of Salem said that her aunt "didn't have an enemy in the world." She had taken up with no male friend after her husband's death and had hosted no "gentlemen callers" or mixed-company parties.

The Crime Reconstruction

The detectives gamed out a sequence of how the horrible crime may have happened.

Ada entered her house at 10:30 p.m. August Olson may or may not have conversed with her till 10:45 p.m. She entered the house alone. She locked the front door. She placed her pocketbook containing five dollars on the dining room table. She went to her room, undressed, got into her kimono nightdress and wound the alarm clock next to her bed. Jeweler Thibault mentioned that the clock by Ada's bedside could run for about thirty hours before needing to be rewound. Thibault estimated that the clock was rewound about seven hours before it stopped at 5:48 a.m., which meant that she rewound it around 10:50 p.m. She went to sleep perhaps around 11:00 p.m.

Was the assailant already hiding in the house? The investigators doubted it.

In the night, the assailant approached the house. The murderer either broke or neatly cut away a portion of the glass pane of the pantry window, permitting him to unlatch the inside sash lock. The murderer then lifted the lower window sash.

The murderer must have been tall, for the latch was almost seven feet from the ground. The murderer must have been strong to lift himself up and through the window. The murderer must have been left-handed, as the cut was located at the top of the bottom left glass pane. The hole permitted him to move the bevel sash lock to an unlocked position.

The murderer lifted the sash and crawled through over the sill, knocking the polish and small china pitcher onto the pantry floor and the Milk of Magnesia bottle to the ground outside.

Ada must have heard something, as she turned on the light and got out of bed. She met her assailant in the hallway, and judging by the blood spatters, that is where the attack began. She turned to flee, and the killer battered the back of her head with a heavy, handheld weapon, crushing the back of her skull and causing a piece of bone to break off and bounce against the wall. She collapsed on the threshold of the adjacent bedroom and bled out.

A photograph of the Johnson house with the pantry window. *From the* Boston Traveler.

Judging by the size of the pool of blood in the hallway, the killer may have spent considerable time in the house.

The killer then carried or dragged Ada's body to the bedroom and placed it on the bed. The killer must have been husky to lift Ada's 160-pound frame.

Did the killer sexually assault Ada? It's reprehensible but possible. Only the autopsy could make this determination.

The murderer lit the bed on fire. State Fire Inspector Trainor believed that no accelerant had been used to hasten the blaze. He was unable to definitively state where exactly the bed was set on fire. The investigators were still open to the idea that the killer had used some sort of flammable liquid to start the blaze. Did the killer search for an accelerant, kerosine for a lantern perhaps? There was no evidence that he did.

It must have taken a while, perhaps an hour, for the fire to spread and increase in intensity to damage the alarm clock on the bedside table. If the clock stopped at 5:48, that would place the time of the fire at 4:48 a.m. Trainor was unable to definitively state when the fire started.

Did the killer ransack anything in a search of valuables? There was no evidence that he did. The pocketbook on the dining room table and the silverware on the sideboard were both untouched.

Did the neighbors hear any commotion or screams? No one interviewed said that they did. Given the cold weather, most neighbors probably had their windows shut. Ada's bedroom window was shut when the firemen broke in the next morning. Strangely enough, all the doors on the second floor were also shut, according to Warren and the firemen's statements. That was strange but fortunate for the house. Closing the door to the bedroom had prevented a draft, which kept the fire smoldering as opposed to becoming a fully developed flashover conflagration.

The murderer left the house through the same pantry window. While exiting, he left smears of blood on the bread container and windowsill. The killer then carefully shut the window. On the turf outside, the killer dropped or left a black pocketbook containing six cents and Ada's electric bill. Investigators wondered if the bag was a plant, a fake clue to make them think robbery was the motive.

The killer's clothes must have been blood-splattered from the attack. He must have taken the weapon he used, probably a hammer, with him. He probably took to the woods behind the home to discard his clothes and weapon. Investigators thought that they had two potential suspects, one a "maniac" from the community. Authorities believed the killer was still at large. Maybe robbery wasn't the motive. There were still a lot of case details that stumped the investigators. But the detectives were confident that they might have a suspect in custody the next day.

Bloody Newspapers
November 1–November 3, 1933

Newspapers printed optimistic reports of bloody newspapers found near Ada Johnson's home. Perhaps the killer had used newsprint sheets to wipe the blood off his hands as he made his getaway. Maybe it was an important clue.

At 10:00 a.m., a search party of five men found a bunch of crumpled Boston newspapers stained with what appeared to be blood in a trash pile to the left of the Johnson house, one hundred feet into the woodland bordered by Pigeon Hill Street, Curtis Street and Oakland Avenue. These men included carpenter Albert Hobbs, Emery Droulette of South Street, William Sears and Harold Holgerson of Curtis Street and Eugene Sullivan, the auto mechanic son of Chief Sullivan. Gene gave the soiled newspapers to his father.

At 11:00 a.m., Holgerson found two more soiled sheets of Boston newspapers. In the afternoon, eight-year-old Harold Pushee of Granite Street found another stained sheet of newspaper in the meadow to the right of the Johnson home, fifty yards from the house.

The newspaper hunt continued on November 2 with an even larger posse of Boy Scouts, high school kids, churchgoers and neighbors. Detective Griffin collected the sheets. He sent them to the state police lab in Boston for chemical analysis. He knew that at least one sheet didn't have human blood, as a local resident mentioned he'd used newspapers to carry the coots he'd shot while out hunting. Other sheets, by their olfactory characteristics, had clearly been used to clean fish.

The next day, the *Gloucester Daily Times* wrote about bloody papers, but it was the *Boston Globe* with the scoop: no human blood had been found on the newsprint. The lead was a bust.

The Diamond Ring
November 1–November 16, 1933

The detectives and the press paid much attention to Ada's diamond ring with the inscription "AJ to AJ" on the inside, which she wore on her left-hand ring finger next to her wedding band at the SCC Halloween party. It was missing. The investigators believed that finding the ring would possibly solve the motive mystery; if it was found at the crime scene, it would eliminate a robbery motive. If it was found somewhere else, it could possibly be traced to the killer. Diamonds and diamond rings were pawnable, and it was easily the most expensive item missing from the crime scene. Perhaps the killer took it as a souvenir.

The problem was that Ada's corpse was missing its left hand, burned off in the fire. The blaze probably melted the wedding band. But where did the diamond ring go?

The investigators did a preliminary search for the ring on the first day of the investigation. Selectman Roy Lane did a more thorough job, first looking on the porch roof and then digging through the remnants of the burnt feather mattress that had been dragged to the backyard. Lane found several finger bones but no ring.

By November 2, investigators had learned more through an interview with Nannie Erickson.

Nannie told investigators that Ada didn't wear her diamond to bed on account of the prongs. Ada took her rings off and kept them in a small china jewelry casket or container on her bedside table. The rings were still missing. The china casket was missing as well.

On the afternoon of November 3, investigators again sifted through the bed debris to find the ring. Detective Griffin sent a teletype to police departments statewide: "Check at all pawn shops for a gold ring, single diamond setting. The ring is missing from the home of the Johnson woman, murdered yesterday in Rockport."

On November 4, Reverend Johanson spoke to the press. He opined that the diamond ring was worth $100. The SCC pastor added, "Johnson was generous....I would not believe that he would have given her any cheap jewelry....Anyone who knew him knew that he would give expensive rings and presents to his wife." State Detectives Griffin and Murray ordered troopers to look for the rings in the debris and ashes. They found nothing.

Boston Post journalist Edwin Inglis commented on the situation on November 8:

> *It looked tonight as if the murder of Mrs. Johnson was a crossword puzzle, a tragic tangle without any definitions, motiveless except for the indication of a missing diamond ring which might have been partially destroyed in the fire, crunched under the heels of firemen and thrown away with the rubbish.*[39]

The next day, there was news. Salem Police Department Inspector Patrick Lehan reported that a diamond ring had been found in the pawnshop owned by Samuel Solomon, the uncle of the recently murdered racketeer and crime boss Charles "King" Solomon. Police brought the ring to Rockport Town Hall. Investigators examined the ring. It did not look like Ada's. Newspapers reported that the man who pawned the ring did so weeks before the murder.

In contrast, the *Boston Traveler* reported that the ring was pawned on November 2 by a "Swedish-looking" man and a woman who kept in the background.

On the afternoon of November 11, State Detective Ferrari, accompanied by State Troopers Harold Peloquin, Robert Jones and E. Barton Thompson Jr., went to Ada's backyard yet to again sift through the carbonized linens, burnt feathers and blacked bedsprings of the mattress, now frozen wet. At 4:00 p.m., Ferrari found Ada's wedding ring. It had not been melted by the fire. He brought the ring back to town hall to give it to Detective Griffin. The plan was to return the next day during daylight to search for the diamond ring. News reports did not mention if that search ever occurred.

In a November 13 press conference, Detective Griffin stated that the investigation team had not given up the search for Ada's diamond solitaire ring. He asked the press to print a message. Anyone who had any information on the missing diamond ring was asked to telephone Rockport-786 to speak to one of the detectives.

In their last update on the subject, newspapers reported on November 16 that the ring was still missing.

Ada's diamond ring has never been found.

An Unlucky Finn
November 2–November 3, 1933

Countless times during the Depression, men stumbled into police stations seeking help. They were cold, starving and desperate. Many were directed to the door, not always gently. Some, however, won a brief respite—a few hours of sleep in a cell, maybe a hot meal or a sandwich. And then, usually, the party ended with a drive out of town and, if they were very lucky, the gift of a dollar or two. They were inevitably told to keep moving.

On the night of November 2, a stocky, unshaven and disheveled middle-aged man, John Luomala (aka Lumola, Luomalo, Lumoia), walked into the Plymouth Police Station, asking for a place to sleep. Manning the night desk was Officer Gault. Gault questioned Luomala but had a hard time understanding the man's broken English and thick Finnish accent. Luomala's story didn't make much sense. He said a woman was following him and seemed frightened, as if he had a persecution complex. Gault was not impressed.

Gault summoned Plymouth Police Chief Russel Dearborn to question the man.

Luomala told Chief Dearborn that he was stonecutter who lived on Saari Parkway in Fitchburg. This turned out to be a fake address. Dearborn again asked Luomala where he lived. Luomala gave out another Fitchburg address, also fake.

Chief Dearborn was not impressed.

Luomala then said that he had stayed with a South Wareham couple the previous Tuesday. Or maybe it was South Carver. He had just walked the six hours to Plymouth to find work, but he was born in Rockport forty-one years prior—or maybe forty-three. He hadn't been back to Rockport for six years—or maybe three. Then he corrected himself again, stating that he was back there the previous Tuesday night. Luomala admitted that he'd been drinking alcohol. Dearborn asked Luomala if he'd heard about the murder of the Rockport woman Ada Johnson.

Luomala replied, "Are you her son?"

Enough. Chief Dearborn took Luomala into custody and then phoned the Essex County DA's Office. The DA's office put Dearborn in touch with Detective Griffin at Rockport Town Hall. Maybe this guy was mentally deranged, but there's something fishy (pun intended) about this Rockporter's November 2 alibi.

Yes, we want to talk to this guy, Griffin said.

Plymouth police took Luomala to the Norwell State Police Barracks. From there, two troopers from the Topsfield Barracks arrived and transported Luomala to Rockport.

Luomala arrived at the Rockport Town Hall at 1:30 a.m. on November 3. Detective Griffin interviewed Luomala for an hour, followed by Detective Murray. Luomala's English was so bad that the detectives had to roust a local Finnish-speaking resident to act as a translator.

Through the volunteer translator, detectives verified that Luomala was an itinerant stonecutter from a Rockport immigrant family. Luomala had last worked as a stone polisher in the Bay View section of town in 1916. He hadn't been back since. He didn't know Ada Johnson. He hadn't even heard of her murder. The detectives tried to force a connection between Luomala and the Hesperus Lunch Cart—but no luck. The detectives turned Luomala over to the Rockport Police, who charged him with vagrancy. Luomala couldn't make bail, so he spent the rest of the night in the station's single cell. He finally got what he had asked for many hours earlier in Plymouth: a place to sleep.

In the morning, a large crowd gathered at town hall. Locals heard about the arrest of Luomala. Detective Griffin asked Sullivan for additional police officers for crowd control.

John Luomala in custody with Rockport and state police officers. *From the* Boston Traveler.

Luomala was arraigned in Gloucester District Court. The detectives explained to Judge York that Luomala had been cleared of suspicion for murder. The vagrancy charge stuck. Since Luomala was clearly homeless, friendless and penniless, Judge York sentenced him to four months in the house of correction for vagrancy. At least over the winter, Luomala would have food, warmth and a bed and would be released in the spring when he could hopefully find a job.

Ada's Autopsy
November 1–November 20, 1933

Ada's autopsy and medical examination is another mystery within a mystery.

At 4:30 p.m. on November 1, undertaker Burgess transported Ada's body to Addison Gilbert Hospital. During the evening, Dr. Ira Hull performed the autopsy, assisted by Dr. William Warren Babson. The two doctors determined the following:

- Ada died of a fractured skull; estimated time of death 5:00 a.m.
- A deep triangular fracture extended from the top of her head to her left ear; one crack was ten centimeters long, and the other was eleven centimeters long. The fracture was an open area where skull was crushed in; parts of the skull had separated, fallen into the hallway and been recovered.
- On one side of the cavity, there was a continuous linear fracture clear to the base of the skull on the right-hand side.
- There were roughly six superficial scalp wounds.
- The brain had contusions and lacerations.
- The weapon used was likely a small, handheld tool with a sharp edge, like a quarry hammer. Her wounds were similar to those found on Arthur Oker's skull.
- With no smoke in her lungs, they were confident that Ada had died before the fire was set.
- Her left hand was burned off, left foot badly charred, left leg badly charred, breasts burnt.
- Ada's right arm, face and right leg were unhurt; the doctors took fingerprints from her right hand.

The doctors were finished by 2:00 a.m. on November 2. Dr. Hull was not willing to provide a specific time of death. The detectives asked Dr. Hull if the victim was "criminally assaulted," the 1930s euphemism for rape. "I cannot tell," Dr. Hull replied.

The state detectives and DA were not happy with that answer. Cregg arranged for Suffolk County Medical Examiner Dr. George Burgess McGrath to be consulted. Dr. McGrath, who had a post at Harvard Medical School, was a famous forensics expert, far more experienced in criminal cases. He would be able to determine if Ada had been sexually assaulted.

Dr. Hull sent the necessary parts of Ada's body to Harvard toxicologist Dr. William F. Boos—by mail. When Cregg heard that, he immediately had the mail package intercepted and returned to Rockport. He then ordered a state trooper to drive the box of body parts to Dr. McGrath's Boston office.

On November 3, the press reported that Dr. McGrath had reviewed Dr. Hull's report and found no evidence in it that would indicate sexual assault. However, Dr. McGrath still had to complete his own research on Ada's body parts, which he had just received.

On November 4, McGrath was supposed to report his medical findings to the anxious DA and state police detectives. For the next several days, McGrath was still working on his report. On November 7, DA Cregg made the cryptic announcement that Dr. McGrath's medical report would not be made public.

On November 20, the *Boston Evening American* reported that Chief Sullivan stated he would continue the investigation under the theory that Ada Johnson was criminally assaulted. The DA never confirmed that the victim was raped. No details of McGrath's report, if he completed it, were ever released.

Ada's Funeral
Friday, November 3, 1933

3:00 p.m.

The Burgess Funeral Home hosted Ada Johnson's funeral. Oscar Johnson, Ada's brother-in-law and a plant engineer for the New England Telephone Company, organized the event. There were perhaps one hundred mourners, with fifty crowding the home's modestly decorated parlor. Detectives and troopers at town hall paused their investigative activities to attend. DA Cregg, Assistant DA Green and Detective Griffin arrived after the service started.

Cregg and Griffin were by the door to the main hall. They watched the mourners attentively.

The service was given in two parts, one in Swedish and one in English. Reverend Johanson read the eulogy in Swedish. In the Swedish eulogy, the reverend did not mention the murder or the connections between the two recent violent deaths in his congregation.

His wife read or extemporized a loose English translation. Mrs. Johnson, whom the *Boston Globe* described as speaking with "eloquence and conviction," said that Ada's death was the outcome of sin and labeled her murder as "foul and inhuman." She mentioned that the community was stunned by the two deaths in the congregation. She said something about God's dark, calamitous events having a silver lining, but they could not yet see any silver lining to this event.

Ada's relatives at her funeral. *From the* Boston Post.

After the eulogies, Mrs. Johanson, perhaps due to a limited repertoire, sang "Someday We'll Understand" and "Shall We Gather At The River."

Journalists described the service as "impressive" said and that the DA and Detective Griffin seemed visibly moved. As the service ended, the detective and DA walked over to the embankment across the street to watch the mourners leave. Bright fall foliage still covered the trees as the gray sky darkened to twilight. State police troopers hovered nearby.

The bereaved then gathered at plot 66 in a corner of Beech Grove Cemetery. There was only one floral arrangement of yellow chrysanthemums on her coffin, so unlike the heaps of flowers placed on her husband's the previous year. The pallbearers—August Olson; Albert and Carl Stolpe, the sons of Ada's sister-in-law; and Carl Strandhal—lowered Ada's coffin into the grave. The reverend recited the committal service and tossed the first handful of dirt onto the casket. Mrs. Johanson sang, this time in Swedish, "Shall We Gather At The River."

The service ended, and the crowd dispersed. Detective Murray mingled among the mourners, and the DA and state troopers stood nearby for these last minutes, scanning the crowd with narrowed eyes, but they saw nothing unusual.

Then the investigators and police left their surveillance and went back to interviewing witnesses. Two gravediggers who had respectfully stood some distance away approached to do their work. Shovelful by shovelful, they covered Ada's coffin with dirt. On the headstone was the name of Ada's husband and his first wife. Ada's name was on it, too, but without a date of death.

Now, that date could be inscribed.

Friday, November 3, 1933

The story in terrified Rockport brought in Boston reporters. Journalist Michael Crawley of the *Boston Traveler* wrote:

> *Looking up from the streets of the town one sees this once quiet little village aglow with the reflection of multi-colored lamps burning brightly in the windows of the many homes until all hours of the night and morning. That the people are thoroughly scared and unable to get their proper rest is evident. Women and children of the neighborhood are intimidated so by fright, that local physicians have had to be summoned on at least three occasions last night to quiet the nerves through a stimulant.*[40]

The *Boston Globe* added:

> "When I went home last night, I found the door of my home shut tight and bolted," John Cooney, a Rockport barber, told the Globe *reporter this afternoon.* "My daughters wouldn't let me in until they saw who I was. They were all worked up over this thing and refused to go out of the house after dark." *He laughed at his daughters' feminine weakness, but added,* "Gosh, I don't know if I blame them."[41]

Ada's neighbor Matilda Anderson told a *Boston Post* reporter that Ada was frightened of robbers and had talked about purchasing a guard dog.

Policemen continued to drag the nearby quarries for evidence. State police continued a house-to-house canvass in the Pigeon Cove neighborhood. They checked several vacated summer homes for squatters. Pigeon Cove residents appealed to Chief Sullivan for a policeman to keep watch in their neighborhood during the night. Sullivan, in turn, appealed to Detective Griffin, who responded that he would see if he could get more troopers.

Investigators speculated that Ada may have struck a blow against her assailant; they based their assumption on a difference in bloodstains at the scene. Maybe the murderer took the weapon from her. The detectives planned to give McGrath blood specimens to see if he could determine differences in blood type.

In the afternoon, detectives stopped by Ada's house to check out the first-floor windows. It struck them as odd that all the windows on the first floor had screens—except for the pantry window. Did this window have a screen? If not, why not? Where did the screen go? It was not inside the house nor outside. Maybe Ada removed it herself. Maybe it was never screened. Maybe the killer took it. Yet more wheels within wheels.

Sergeant Toelken reported that in another area of the house, he found a print that matched one lifted from the Milk of Magnesia bottle. Cregg wanted fingerprints taken of twenty neighbors in the Pigeon Hill area. All twenty matched the investigator's hunches about the size and strength of the attacker, although it's not clear if they were all tall and left-handed. In the evening, investigators had collected prints from eight of the individuals. But Cregg conceded that several persons had entered the home via the pantry window after the discovery of the fire. (Didn't anyone think to unlock the door?) However, he was confident he could find a match between the prints from the crime scene and the prints of the neighbors.

The Essex County Commissioners replied to the Rockport Selectmen regarding the county offering a reward for the apprehension of Ada Johnson's murderer. They had no authority under state law to offer one. They suggested that the town try the DA's office, which, in their opinion, had sufficiently implied lawful authority and that the commissioners would support such an approach. Newspapers published the text of the reply.

Rockport Police got word of a teen party in the Sheep Pasture area on the night of the murder. The kids had partied with booze until 1:00 a.m., so they thought the party had broken up hours before Johnson was attacked. There was nothing of value in that tale.

Investigators conducted up to forty witness interviews that day. Police questioned Otto Reiss, forty, a rubbish wagon driver. Reiss had done some work for both Oker and Johnson. They cleared Reiss of suspicion when he explained that he hadn't done any work for Ada in over a year and hadn't seen her since then. The DA interviewed stoneworker Roscoe Ricker, who supposedly had a hot tip. It turned out Ricker didn't. Cregg, Griffin and Murray questioned Peter Hill, a kid from Lanesville who had done a stint in the Salem Jail for breaking and entering into a local grocery store in

July 1932. Hill's criminal record and six-foot-one-inch height made him a suspect. Hill was cleared.

August Olson was interviewed again. August recalled chatting about church affairs with Ada about 10:45 p.m. but only for a few minutes.

A guy named Otto Erickson came into town hall with an odd story.[42] He was at 2 Orchard Avenue on November 1 at 8:30 a.m., when Warren entered the house and the fireman arrived. When Warren came out of the house, he neglected to tell the fireman there was a body in the burning bedroom. The firemen found out soon enough, but Olson's omission struck this witness as being something he should report. It explained why newspapers carried conflicting reports about who found Ada's body, Olson or the firefighters.

Detectives asked Warren Olson to appear for questioning; he missed Ada's funeral because he was stuck in town hall waiting to be interviewed. The investigators opened by saying that they had a couple questions about the fire and the discovery of Ada's body. Detective Griffin and Sergeant Toelken asked Warren to re-create how he got into the house and what he did afterward. Warren showed them. They asked about the shoes he wore in the house. "I wore slippers," Warren replied, "but my mom asked me to burn them. They were all bloody and ruined, so I did." The *Boston Post* later reported about the destroyed slippers and the curious fact that Warren worked at the A&P store next to Oker's shop back in May 1932. Detective Griffin clarified that Warren was not a suspect.[43]

The DA spent a long time chatting with Reverend Johanson. Inspectors took the cleric's fingerprints. Cregg pressed him about his congregants and his church events: "Something goes on at those meetings, or something occurs which arouses the passion to slay in this blood-lusty creature we seek." Johanson refused to believe that a member of his congregation could be the murderer but admitted that the killer had deep knowledge of the activities of the church and its members, including the surprise Halloween party. He brought up an event from the past that might have bearing on the matter.

That night, law enforcement officials held another press conference. The case seemed, as the *Gloucester Times* reported, at a "standstill." Detective Murray told reporters that they believed a member of the local Swedish community murdered Ada Johnson. Yet troopers looked in deserted homes for squatters. Some journalists doubted the connection to the Oker case; investigators thought they were connected, but Detective Griffin tersely added, "We haven't eliminated any theory—or anybody." The investigators spoke elliptically of a potential suspect, a *Dr. Jekyll and Mr. Hyde*–type character. But there was not enough evidence against anybody to make an arrest. Plus, there was the reverend's strange story and the rumors that Ada was being stalked by a dirty old man.

Dirty Old Man
November 2–November 4, 1933

Investigators wanted to know if Ada had any relations with member of the opposite sex. Was anyone interested in her? Could she have refused a man's advances, provoking a vicious reprisal, murder a result of unrequited lust? Two "spurned suitor" candidates came in for questioning. One was a man in his fifties, married with three kids, who was not a member of the SCC. The other was a seventy-five-year-old man. Miss Hazel Johnson of New Bedford, Massachusetts, had interesting stories about them.

Hazel was the attractive teenage niece of Ada from New Bedford who occasionally visited her aunt in Rockport. Hazel recounted that on the evening of her last visit, she and her aunt were followed by a "stocky man" on the street. She told a *Boston Post* reporter:

> *I visited my aunt in Rockport last August. On two successive nights we went out for a walk. Both nights a man, about 60 years old and of stocky build, followed us. I didn't think much about it the first night, but the second night I asked my aunt who he was. My aunt said she didn't know the man and that she was afraid of him, too. She told me at that time that she caught him looking in through one of the windows of the kitchen of her home a short time before. The man ran away from the house, my aunt said, when he saw her looking at him.*[44]

Hazel's father and aunt, Oscar Johnson and Mrs. Anna Stolpe, corroborated Hazel's story and added grown-up details. The man had apparently been "at odds" with Ada Johnson for three years. Mrs. Stolpe told investigators that Ada told her that several mornings—Ada was an early riser, often in her kitchen at 6:00 a.m. making breakfast—the man would suddenly appear at her pantry window, asking to be let in.

Once, when Ada and Hazel were sitting on the porch at Oakland Avenue, this man trespassed onto Ada's lawn and attempted conversation. Ada demanded that he get off the property. The man said to Ada, "You can be had. You'll be nice to me, one way or another....I'll date you up yet."

There was a rumor in town that the man snuck into the house and crawled into Ada's bed, but that was a gossipy tall tale.

Although Hazel's story and the subsequent press reports conflated the two men, detectives focused on the older man as the likelier—or at least creepier—suspect. Ms. Stolpe gave the man's name and address to Detective Griffin, and he paid a visit to the dirty old man.

The man denied hassling Ada. The detective responded, "We know it was you. If you keep denying it, we'll bring in a witness that can identify you."

The man said something like, "Hey, I was just joshing—didn't mean nuthin' by it."

The detective responded, "If you don't tell me the full truth, after I get the witness to ID you as Ada's stalker, we'll book you on suspicion of murder."

It's not clear what happened next; there may have been a search for a weapon or bloodstained clothing in the man's cellar. The man folded and recanted his prior denials. In the end, the dirty old man was cleared as a suspect.

The Pistol-Packing Pastor

Investigators heard a wild tale from Reverend Johanson that needed follow-up. The reverend had spoken about it to Chief Sullivan and several reporters but not the state detectives. After Ada Johnson's funeral, DA Cregg asked the cleric to come see him.

The incident had occurred almost two years before, when the reverend was only two weeks into his tenure as pastor of the SCC. The following merged account of his baffling encounter came from Reverend Johanson, as printed in the *Lynn Daily Item* and the *Boston Traveler*:

> The attack occurred as I stepped off the midnight train. I had been to Boston at a theatrical party/church meeting.[45] As I started away from the station this man, swarthy and heavy, leaped at me from an ambush and struck me a heavy blow. "You're out too late," he hissed into my ear, and there was a fiendish note, indescribably cold, in his voice. It seemed like the voice of a demon or a maniac. I dodged his blows and pulled myself away from him. I ran and he chased me, but I got away. Since that time I have learned the identity of my assailant. I'm quite certain. He lives in

Rockport, he is an American and is not a member of my congregation. I never told police because I feared reprisal if I did so.[46]

"I still fear for my life," Johanson told Cregg.

The reverend told newspapers that the next day, he took out a concealed carry permit and went to a jeweler's store to repair the trigger of his .38 revolver. New accounts varied about whether the pastor was still packing. It is unknown if the issue came up in his discussion with Cregg.

Investigators determined that the reverend's attack story had no bearing on the case.

Reverend Harrald, Drama Mamma

Reverend Waldemar Harrald, former SCC pastor and current superintendent of the Scandinavian Sailors Home in East Boston, told journalists that he had information which might help the police. "Something happened several years ago which I have pondered over since this horrible murder," said Harrald on the record. "I cannot reveal it because I feel a grave injustice may be done to the entire family. However, if the police ask me anything I will tell them what I know."

The press wanted to know more. The investigators took note. Harrald had been in place to receive confidences from troubled people and to learn secrets, often dark ones, as part of his ministry. What sort of secrets could Harrald spill?

The reverend told his tales. Back when he was SCC pastor in the mid- to late 1920s, he saw a man trying to steal clothes from his backyard clothesline. He mentioned rumors of a Peeping Tom sneaking about the Pigeon Cove area. He brought up a Rockport man from a family of "fine people" but who "drank considerably." The man had made a "fresh overture" to Ada but had been easily rebuffed. Harrald mentioned that at the time, the weight of the incident had been accorded "slight" importance.

Harrald's bombshell turned out to be a damp squib. Investigators eliminated the clothesline thief as a person of interest. The reverend's press interviews did produce some memorable quotes, however. On the SCC, he commented:

Too much stress has been placed on the church. No member of that church should be under suspicion. I would trust them with a million dollars if I had it. It may be that there is a maniac lurking in the woods, or living in a shack. You know that there are 14 miles of woods nearby.[47]

Harrald had this to say about Rockport's Nordic community:

You know, Finnish and Swedish people will fight; they will draw a knife, but they will never kill.

Saturday, November 4, 1933

The newspapers, after calling the crime a "torch slaying" and "cleaver murder," settled on calling the perpetrator the "Rockport Maniac." The press and the public pressured the authorities to solve the crime. It was now the fourth day of the investigation.

At 10:00 a.m., the district attorney conferenced with the entire investigative team in town hall. Present were the DA, Assistant DA Green, Detectives Griffin and Murray, a half-dozen state troopers, plus the Rockport Police. The team then broke up, with police and state troopers continuing their search in the Sheep's Pasture, Pigeon Hill and Pigeon Cove neighborhoods for evidence. Their orders were to be especially on the lookout for a "facing hammer," the handheld bush hammer used by stonecutters.

The detectives and DA began with the day's slate of interviews, fourteen in total. Investigators used the same set of questions from a "stereotyped" interview form for each witness. Several of the witnesses were fingerprinted. The first session was a second interview with August Olson. Olson pointed out that Ada's two brothers and a sister in Rockford, Illinois, were still unaware of her death. No one in the SCC or in Rockport had their address. Detectives promised to contact Rockford Police to locate them.

They interviewed a Boston-based man, described as a nephew of Mrs. Johnson, who had been "down and out" after the death of her husband. Ada gave the nephew some clothes, and he stayed at her house for a while. Another victim of the Depression, he was cleared as a suspect.

The Rockport Selectmen were disappointed at the refusal by the Essex County Commissioners to post a reward. DA Cregg pondered making an official request to Governor Ely. Perhaps he would be willing to pony up state monies for the capture and conviction of the murderer.

Sergeant Toelken of the state police crime lab had disappointing news. The fingerprint on the Milk of Magnesia bottle didn't match any from the Oker crime scene. He would keep at the tedious work to see if the print on the bottle matched any from the Johnson house. It was not looking good. The Oker crime scene fingerprint evidence was tainted, as a bunch of random people had touched all sorts of surfaces. Even the Milk of Magnesia bottle was not a sure-fire piece of evidence. Yes, Toelken had gotten a single print from it, but there were other prints and smears that were difficult if not impossible to lift. The bottle had lain on the damp ground for hours on November 1 and had apparently been handled multiple times before it was obtained as evidence. The Johnson crime scene itself, between the firemen, the police, the fire itself and the crowd-sourced volunteer crew of investigators, was likely tainted as well.

Reverend Johanson gave an interview with the press in which he described his flock as being livid over articles published in the "cosmopolitan dailies," insinuating a connection between their church and the murders. He commented:

> *I cannot believe that the murderer is one of my congregation. We have but 20 men in the church. They are but a third of the entire membership. I know every one of them, and it is ridiculous to hint that any one of them is a fiend, but it is certainly someone who knows all the churchgoers well, I will admit.... The murderer of Mrs. Johnson may have been a sex-mad man, but I am more inclined to the belief that she was slain by a burglar, I have gone into it very carefully, and I am certain there can be no motive of revenge. She was a kindly soul and no one could have borne her any grudge whatsoever.*[48]

Johanson said that his congregation asked him to write a strongly worded letter protesting the reporting, especially the accounts of the surprise Halloween party and the eight male members who attended it. He claimed that new reports of the midnight meeting with the DA were overblown; Cregg simply asked for the congregation's cooperation and for them to offer whatever information they could. The reverend adamantly clarified that Ada Johnson did not take part in church activities and was not a member of the SCC.

When asked if he would talk about the murder at his upcoming service, he mentioned that he would not discuss it. "We Swedes stick pretty close to the gospel," he tersely replied. Going back to the robbery angle, the reverend mentioned that Warren Olson told him that he heard footsteps outside Ada Johnson's house the night of the murder.

Late in the day, Selectman Roy Lane visited with the state troopers in town hall. After a closed-door session, Detective Griffin and Assistant DA Green left Rockport on a mysterious errand. Newspapermen speculated that they were off to interview and possibly arrest a suspect.

Cregg and the detectives held a press conference at the end of the day. Investigators were certain the killer was a resident of the community or a person well-known in the community. They had a list of neighbors who had shaky alibis for Halloween night. They were looking at the height and weight of persons of interest as possible qualifiers. Cregg commented, "The case of Mrs. Johnson grips me like no other crime I have ever encountered. We are convinced that a fiendish killer of *Jekyll and Hyde* complex is abroad in this community."

Cregg admitted they were no closer to apprehending the killer. But they did mention—as later reported by the *Boston Traveler*—that they found inconsistencies in the story told by one person of interest which might indicate progress.

A newsman asked for a comment about the reports from the SCC pastor that Warren Olson heard a prowler outside Ada's house the night of the murder: "No, young Mr. Olson said he heard a car drive by but nothing about footsteps. We'll question him again. Maybe the reverend was mistaken in his interpretation of the story." The *Boston Herald* would later comment on the natural reticence of the Swedish community. The *Boston Globe* commented that this was "the most intensive manhunt Cape Ann has ever witnessed."

That intensity would increase.

Warren Olson and Reverend Johanson. *From the* Boston Daily Record.

Sunday, November 5, 1933

For a week, Rockport residents applied for firearms permits at a record clip. The town clerk gave a pistol permit to every Rockporter who applied as long as they had no criminal record. The clerk was also inundated with dog license applications. For some reason, everybody wanted a guard dog.

State troopers from the Reading and Topsfield Barracks canvassed the Pigeon Hill neighborhood, with a quota of twenty-five houses to visit. State detectives were certain that the killer's clothes must have been blood-soaked, and the perpetrator must have tossed the soiled garments away.

Detectives had prepared a standardized notetaking form for the troopers to use during their interviews. Each form, printed on glossy paper to pick up fingerprints, included spaces for the subject's name and address and space for notetaking by the trooper with two questions:

- "Is anyone missing from your household?"
- "Has any member stopped wearing his normal apparel?"

After the interview, residents were required to sign the form. At the end of each day, all the forms would be sent to the state police headquarters at the state house for analysis. The *Boston Post* reported, "This procedure breaks all precedent in the handling of murder cases in Massachusetts and shows the determination of the authorities to use every possible method to trap the killer."

With the (probably unenthusiastic) collaboration of the pastor, the DA prepared a questionnaire to be given to each member of the SCC. This questionnaire was designed by Cregg to be a "psychological test" to uncover evidence.

Reverend Johanson's 10:00 a.m. service was a generic take on All Souls Day given in Swedish. Detectives Murray and Griffin and Assistant DA Green attended the service to hand out the questionnaire and watch congregants' behaviors. Members of the press attended as well. Newsmen and investigators perhaps outnumbered congregants, of which only fifteen appeared. Reverend Johanson commented that most of his flock had been frightened away with all the talk of a killer among them.

After church, Detectives Murray and Griffin and Assistant DA Green interviewed ten people at town hall. A woman told Detective Griffin that she dreamt of a man chasing Ada Johnson through the woods and then clubbing her on the head. They investigated a report of a hiker with a walking stick who lurked around the woods near Johnson's house a week before the murder. The team cross-referenced each Pigeon Hill resident's alibi and what each said about the other. They mulled over bothersome aspects of the case—how much time the killer spent in the house and the fact that all the second-floor doors were shut and the pantry window was pulled down. Toelken's fingerprint report wasn't ready, but detectives were hopeful with his finding two fingerprints on the inside sill of the pantry window. If only the crime scene wasn't such a mess.

The most important action that Sunday was another session with Warren Olson. There were things he said and didn't say about Halloween night that the investigation team wanted clarification on. Warren had previously told investigators that he heard a car go down Stockholm Avenue at 4:00 a.m. That checked out—Stockholm Avenue resident John Mattson mentioned that he left in his car to go pheasant hunting at that time and saw nothing amiss at the Johnson house. But what was this story about hearing a burglar, the one Olson told the reverend about and that he mentioned to the newspapers?

Olson clarified his story. No doubt his face and gestures, his voice and tone were all closely observed as he explained.

He got back from driving partygoers home at 11:00 p.m. His parents were in their bedroom, presumably asleep. He went to the kitchen because he still had a task to complete; he needed to paint text on signs for the upcoming Ladies Aid Society concert the following Wednesday. He sat at the kitchen table to work on the signs.

Sometime after midnight, he heard a loud *clump*! It sounded like a jump or a tramp of a heavy footfall on the lawn across the street, a noise so loud that he got up from the kitchen table to look out the kitchen window. He wandered through the first floor, peering out several windows. He did not see anyone, nor did he hear any more noises.

He returned to the kitchen table and worked on lettering until 1:00 a.m., when he went to bed. At 4:00 a.m., he was briefly awakened by the sound of a passing automobile. He fell back asleep until around 8:15 a.m., when Carne's shouts and door pounding woke him up and he came downstairs.

The detectives asked about the sequence of events during the discovery of the fire. When did you enter the pantry window? How did you get in? Like his father, Olson was short, only about five feet, six inches tall. What did you tell the firemen when they arrived? We heard the smoke was so thick on the second floor—did you go up there? Who slipped on the blood on the floor of the hallway? When did you slip out of the pantry window?

The detectives asked about his destroyed footwear. When did your mother tell you to burn your slippers? When were the slippers destroyed? Did you burn them, or did your mother burn them?

After three hours of questioning, the investigation team let Olson go. He had been, in their words, of "considerable assistance" to their efforts. They liked working with Olson because he was familiar with the layout of Ada's house and grounds prior to the fire and the trampling of the grounds by onlookers. The discussion produced no breaks in the case but was helpful. Olson remained, as the *Boston Evening American* stated in a photograph caption from the previous day's edition, "freed of all suspicion."[49]

Olson would later tell a *Gloucester Daily Times* reporter that the sound he heard Halloween night wasn't a prowler. It was just a thudding sound. He heard no footsteps. He saw no shadow. It was late, and he was probably working too hard.

It was a gorgeous fall afternoon. Curious onlookers in their cars caused a traffic jam on Stockholm Avenue. Up to two hundred morbidly curious souls gathered outside Ada Johnson's house, gawking at the soot smudge by her bedroom window, the infamous pantry window and the other windows that gaily displayed potted plants and flowers inside.

The SCC evening service was better attended. Thirty women and girls along with ten men listened to a desultory and depressing message delivered, as always, in Swedish and English. No detectives were present, only journalists. Mrs. Johanson provided a translation of the sermon "Thou Shalt Not Kill." Johanson's sermon mentioned that the murderer would be punished in a future life, that justice belonged to the Lord and that the congregation should aid the investigators in any way that they could. He said that people were using the murders to "blacken the church" but that it "will stand in spite of it all." Johanson exclaimed, "I pray to God that the problem of this crime will be solved!"

The *Boston Globe* reported on the town's atmosphere:

> *Police walked the narrow winding streets of Pigeon Cove tonight to reassure uneasy townspeople. Lights burn all night in many homes since the Johnson murder, and doors are bolted tight the minute the sun goes down. Women no longer walk even a short distance to a neighbor's house alone. Fear is in the community, and judging from the way townsfolk talk, that fear will remain until the killer is arrested.*[50]

The DA made an announcement at the evening press conference. There were five male suspects under consideration, all Rockporters. One was a prominent member of the Swedish Pigeon Cove community. Two others were members of the SCC. They "linked by a strong circumstantial chain" to Oker's murder. Some suspects had been questioned at length, others not. Their alibis had raised suspicions. They were under surveillance. Cregg stated:

> *Unless the situation changes materially, one of the five men under investigation will be under arrest by tomorrow. The man I have in mind has talked so much as to indicate that he was almost an eyewitness to the crime, and he will be held as a material witness, at least.*[51]

Detective Griffin declared that he was "all done being nice to these five men....I'm going to bear down on them and sweat the truth out of them."

Cregg continued that the press and the people of Rockport would be shocked at the news of the arrest of the subject. The *Post* reported that the suspect was:

> *A man bearing one of the most irreproachable characters in the village. He is known to have had opportunity in each of the murders. At the mere mention of his name, detectives have met with explanations of the man's virtues. The State officers believe that it would be foolhardy, in view of the array of defense which has been thrown about this man, to grill him at present.*[52]

Cregg declared that the suspect was undoubtedly "conceited enough to believe himself secure, and it is this over-confidence which may be the means of his undoing."

Monday, November 6, 1933

The day was freezing cold with the occasional flurry. Investigators relocated their headquarters from the selectmen's office to the second floor of the town hall so the selectmen could continue their official duties unimpeded. It would also help the detectives avoid the newspapermen, constantly underfoot in the public building looking for a scoop. Journalists were everywhere in town now, wandering the streets and docks, poking around in woods, quarries and cellar holes.

The DA was expected to drop by Rockport. He wanted to "speed up" the investigation. The detectives felt the pressure. They were particularly interested in reports of people who had left town recently. There was one lead from Portland, Maine. Police there had picked up a suspicious man who said he'd left Rockport the previous Sunday. Detective Griffin asked the Portland Police to question the man and report back if there was any connection to the Rockport murder.

The investigators sent out an all-points bulletin to try to find that Bible salesman who attended the Halloween party. The salesman apparently skipped town "about five minutes" after the murder was discovered (according to the *Boston Daily Record*).

Uniformed state police troopers continued their door-to-door canvass. The plan was for all Finnish and Swedish families in the Pigeon Cove section to be interviewed. Heads of households had to account for the movements of all their family members on Halloween night.

The *Gloucester Day Times* ran an article on the links between the Johnson and Oker cases, briefly touching on Rockport's last murder in 1877. The paper confirmed the allegations of the tainted Oker crime scene:

> *Criticism has been made of the Rockport police in not keeping the curious from the shop that noon so as to preserve finger-prints and other evidence. But those who so criticize, fail to realize that the officer who first arrived on the scene was told by the doctor that there was still a faint spark of life in Oker, and knowing that, the officer sensed that his first duty was to get that man to a hospital where he could be properly attended. He was along and bent all his energy towards that purpose.*[53]

The article also mentioned that the moon was full the day Oker was killed. Readers were quick to realize that the Johnson killing occurred just before the November 2 full moon. A new nickname for the cases, the "Full of the Moon Murders," was born.

Geoffrey Parsons Jr. of the *Boston Globe* wrote:

> *Townsfolk—Yankees, Swedes and Finns—have abandoned the close-mouthed characteristics attributed to them, and have poured into the willing ears of the police all kinds of tales, rumors, reports and suspicions....Six days have elapsed since the murder was committed, and the townspeople are clamoring for action on the part of the police. Their nerves are worn ragged from the thought that the murderer is still at large in their midst, and they want something done by the police.*[54]

Parsons reported that the investigators were reinterviewing four people that day, out of the scores questioned, and that state investigators had "narrowed down their list of suspects to the point where their suspicions fall overwhelmingly on one man." He continued:

> *The man the police suspect of the murder has an impeccable reputation in the Pigeon Cove community in which he lives. He is a regular church-goer, and from all outward appearances a model citizen. Whenever his name is mentioned in the community it arouses words of praise, of friendliness. There is no police record lurking in the background of his life. He is described as a daily reader of the Bible by his friends and neighbors....If and when the police decide to ask for a warrant for his arrest for the brutal murder of Mrs. Johnson, this town will be terribly shocked. The character of* Dr. Jekyl [sic] and Mr. Hyde *will be made very real to them.*[55]

An arrest at day's end was conceivable.

Detectives reinterviewed William Carne, the man who pulled the fire alarm the morning of November 1. Detectives reinterviewed Reverend and Mrs. Albert M. Johanson for almost two hours. The pastor shared information. The investigators had heard it all before. Whatever it was, the news was not disclosed to the press.

Warren Olson was working at his clerk job at the A&P store in downtown Rockport when state troopers Frank Byrne and William Faron arrived. The officers escorted Warren to town hall. There, Assistant DA Charles Green and State Detectives Griffin and Murray interviewed Warren for over three hours. This was the fourth and longest interview that investigators had done with Warren. Detectives had still more questions about his most recent testimony, as yet again, Warren had responded with conflicting statements in his previous session. The investigators grilled Warren over what one paper later described as "the most intimate details of his life and the knowledge of Pigeon Cove affairs." Another paper mentioned how his daylight detention caused a sensation in town. It was common knowledge that Warren's father succeeded Arthur Oker as the SCC church president. After the interrogation, troopers escorted Warren back to the store.

The detectives visited Ada Johnson's house and removed some paperwork. They then went to Oker's tailor shop,

State troopers and Rockport Police escort Warren Olson to his fourth questioning. *From the* Boston Post.

now run by his son Rudolph. They talked to Rudolph for a while and inspected the interior of the shop.

Cregg later told reporters that the Warren interrogation had reduced the number of suspects in the investigator's sights from five to three, all of whom were neighbors of Ada Johnson. Warren had, according to one paper, cleared up some outstanding questions and "eliminated suspicions they had entertained for several days regarding the identity of the slayer." Detective Griffin commented, "Olson's story cleared up several important points about which we had been doubtful."

There was not enough evidence to merit an arrest yet. The investigators still believed that the murderer must have had bloody clothes and the weapon, and he must have disposed of both. If they could not find the bloodstained clothes or a weapon, perhaps they could find someone who saw the killer attempting to dispose of the evidence.

That evening, investigators took a break and attended the Rockport Firemen's Association steamed clam supper at Hook and Ladder Hall over the police station. Journalists were invited as well. The *Gloucester Daily Times* described it as a "jolly affair."

The Pantry Prowler
November 4–November 8, 1933

On November 4, Mrs. Frances Griffith of 36 Pigeon Hill Street reported the theft of a pound of butter from the ice chest on her back porch. It was the Depression, a time when theft was common, so police were not interested. It wasn't like a killer in the woods could survive the cold on a pound of butter.

Then it happened again. Around November 6, Mrs. Griffith saw a strange man peering into her window around 5:30 p.m. Her husband ran upstairs to grab a pistol, but by the time he got to the porch, the man was gone. Investigators noted the reports that strange men had been seen peering into windows round the Pigeon Hill neighborhood. But investigators had spent a lot of time peering into windows in the neighborhood recently.

On November 7, Mrs. Griffith again called the cops. She had come home shortly after dark to find a kitchen window screen missing, wrenched from its sash, which was now broken. The window was open. Someone had stolen a quart of milk and a bottle of buttermilk.

This was not good.

Detective Griffin, Rockport Police and state troopers took three cruisers to her house. The police searched the neighborhood but found nothing. Detectives interviewed Frances Griffith, a chemist who worked at the Gloucester Fish Laboratory. The investigators took part of the broken window sash back to town hall to dust it for fingerprints. Sergeant Toelken took samples and reported that he could find no fingerprints on the outside of the sash; there were prints only on the inside. He noted that the intruder had to remove three screws placed in the window to wrench it open.

On November 8, Frances Griffith conferred with investigators at town hall. To help police find the missing window screen, he brought the other kitchen window screen with him. Investigators learned something interesting. They already knew, of course, that his residence was only 150 feet from Ada Johnson's house. But they learned that back in 1932, the Griffiths rented an apartment at 77 Main Street, directly above Arthur Oker's shop. Detectives wondered if the killer was targeting the couple, who lived adjacent to both of Rockport's recent murders.

The DA offered police protection to the Griffiths. It is unclear if this was done or how long the protection lasted. The newspapers reported that Mr. Griffith had a "small arsenal" of firearms at home. No more burglaries occurred. The larder coverage faded altogether from the headlines.

The Babson Farm Ghost Hunt
November 5–November 6, 1933

On Sunday, investigators heard a strange story.

Back in June, Dr. Earl Green of Rockport had gotten a call to visit a dilapidated farmhouse, nicknamed the "Babson Farm," between Folly Cove and Orchard Avenue. There was a hysterical man; he needed help. The farmhouse had been abandoned by its owner because it was supposedly haunted. Dr. Green headed to the house to see what the matter was.[56]

A group of itinerant orchestra musicians who were on tour were squatting there. They said that they had been playing pranks on each other. One musician took the mattress of another musician and tossed it into the cellar via a trapdoor in the floor. The other musician went down the hole to retrieve it. He was down there for a bit and then started screaming. The other musicians let him out of the cellar. The guy said that he was attacked and choked by someone in the cellar with "monstrous strength." The other musicians didn't

Burgess and Moody investigating the Babson Farm cellar. *From the* Boston Post.

see anyone in the cellar. The man was incoherent, inconsolable, "one of the worst cases of fright I have ever seen," commented the doctor.

Investigators weren't sure what to make of it. Maybe the musician accidentally stumbled onto a hiding rumrunner. They knew that "hobos," the homeless and bootleggers used abandoned houses. Perhaps the killer did, too.

On Monday, November 6, Gloucester Police Officers Burgess and Moody checked out the farmhouse. They went into the cellar. They found old wine bottles, bottle caps and broken lanterns. They found a "tunnel" as part of the substructure. But they did not find any ghosts, bootleggers or maniac murderers.

Where There Is Smoke, There Are Saunas
November 5–November 7, 1933

It was only a matter of time before a reporter with time on their hands and space to fill found their way to publicize that exotic institution: the Scandinavian bathhouse, i.e. the sauna. Saunas were openly accessible. There were over a dozen in Rockport and Lanesville, where guests could sweat for a few coins. Many more households had saunas just for the family, at which nothing hotter than a heated bath was taking place. Steamy scenes could be imagined but only by ignorant city folks. There was also the angle of Nordic nude bathing on Rockport's beaches. The question of how salacious an imaginative reporter could make their story was answered by William Brawthers of the *Boston Daily Record*.

The exposé lasted only a daily news cycle before facts poured cold water on it. Yes, there were bathhouses, but mixed sauna soakers were strictly limited to family members only. Otherwise, the bathing was strictly segregated by gender. There was no evidence Ada ever visited a bathhouse. As for nude sunbathing on the beaches, yes it happened occasionally. But the Finns and Swedes were respectable, discreet; the Rockport Police had never had a complaint. Ada wasn't the nude sunbathing type either.

Investigators did hear of one odd aspect to the story. They heard a report that on the morning of Wednesday, November 1, there was smoke coming from one of the bathhouses' chimneys. They asked one of the two sauna caretakers—possibly a Finn named John Mattson—about it. He thought it odd as well. Finns usually took their baths on Saturdays. Besides, the baths had been closed for the past three weeks.

Odd indeed.

Tuesday, November 7, 1933

Journalists ran stories on the previous day's interviews. The *Boston Globe* reported that the man who was the leading contender "virtually eliminated himself as a suspect." The *Boston Evening American* wrote:

> *When they had finished questioning young Olson, the State detectives in charge of the investigation indicated that on the basis of additional information that they had obtained from him they would virtually have to drop the suspicions they had entertained for several days regarding the possible identity of the killer.*

The investigative team finished moving their headquarters from the selectmen's office to the second-floor auditorium. There, the team had room and were further insulated from the journalists and photographers, who wandered not just the streets of Rockport but also the halls of the public building. The Rockport Selectmen could have their office back. In the morning, Detective Griffin interviewed SCC member and handyman

Carl Strandhal, the administrator of Ada's chickens and canary. Griffin asked Strandhal about Ada's habits and customs in the weeks leading up to her death.

Journalists and investigators focused their attentions on men who had left town. Three Rockport men had left the area in the past week, one on the day of the murder and two others on November 4. Nothing specifically connected them to the crime—yet. Detectives asked for the assistance of the Boston Police Department to track down a Rockport man who had recently been seen in Boston. Cregg and detectives interviewed a Saugus man who worked at a company that sold bakery goods door to door. Halloween was his first day on the job, and his assigned sales route was Rockport. He went door to door peddling his bread, rolls and doughnuts until 6:00 p.m. He was picked up for questioning and quickly released.

The *Gloucester Daily Times* asked Rudolph Ranta, a sign painter on Forest Street, to get in touch with authorities. Ranta had left town the previous Wednesday by train, headed for Boston. He got off at the Manchester station and then got a ride from a resident named Mark Cochrane to Charlestown. Ranta told Cochrane he was heading to Albany to look for a job. He had left multiple forwarding addresses with relatives, who frankly didn't know where he was. Police assured the *Gloucester Daily Times* that Ranta was no more a suspect than anyone else in town. Of course, in a town where everyone was a suspect, that was little comfort.

When they were not hounding AWOL Rockport men, both investigators and journalists explored abandoned shacks and vestigial tunnels. They looked wherever a killer might hide and checked all the holes, chasms, motions and quarries into which the killer may have tossed bloody clothing or the murder weapon. If the killer had tossed a hammer into a quarry, it would likely never be found, but clothing floats. Or perhaps the negative could be a key piece of evidence—a citizen would notice that a neighbor no longer wore their favorite suit, for example. But there were no bloodstains on the stone wall between the Johnson property and the adjacent woodlot, heading to the quarries. The lack of evidence was maddening.

The police had fielded a lot of wacky stories. Psychics and charlatans phoned the station claiming to have preternatural knowledge of the murders from their dreams and visions. There were reports of lights flashing on and off at the Johnson house. Officers wondered if people were just seeing things.

That afternoon, the DA reviewed the case with the consolidated investigation team. He then met with the Rockport Selectmen. They discussed the reward money and the possibility of enacting more extreme measures to apprehend the killer. The selectmen began drafting a statement.

At that evening's press conference, Detective Griffin assured reporters that there was no letup in the investigation. Geoffrey Parsons Jr. of the *Boston Globe* filed a dispatch that day, with the observation, "No arrest has been made and police admit that they have no real suspect in sight, or out of sight, for that matter." He continued:

> *With virtually no vital or significant evidence to work on, investigators are confronted with an extraordinarily baffling crime. A thoroughly respectable woman, living alone, is murdered for no apparent reason in a normally law-abiding community. The murder resembles another, still unsolved, which shocked Rockport 17 months ago. That is about all police actually have to work on.*[57]

The *Gloucester Daily Times* reported:

> *There are some of the opinion that the fiend has concluded his bestial mission, having satisfied the motive for which he slew two residents within 18 months. They have concluded that the fiend was quite sane in his actions but was moved by fierce emotions that had been nurtured through months of apparently calm and solid demeanor until the storm of passion within him arose to that zenith that demanded the life of his victim against whom he had a very definite reason for his secret hatred.*[58]

Wednesday, November 8, 1933

The day's plan was for the four state troopers involved in the case to canvass the forests north of Pigeon Cove. There were scores of deserted shacks, tool sheds, cellar holes and dormant quarries to search. The investigators' latest theory was that the killer was hiding somewhere close by, emerging at night to steal food, although Detective Griffin himself was apparently not convinced the murderer was hiding in the wilds of Cape Ann. Troopers brought in a hammer, an old brown coat and a ceramic coffee mug to town hall. Detective Griffin declined to explain the significance, if any, of the items.

Cognizant of the attention he drew whether he spoke or stood silent, Reverend Johanson issued a statement that he and his wife were willing to cooperate to catch the "demoniacal slayer" and volunteered to help troopers search the Pigeon Cove woods. They stated, "We earnestly hope and pray for a gleam of light in this mystery and that this fiendish crime be justly punished, ensuring peace and safety once more to our quaintly beautiful village."

There was a rumor that Sergeant Toelken would give his fingerprint findings report to the investigation team on November 8. This report was false. The lab man did not appear.

Massachusetts State Police Detective Joseph Ferrari joined the investigation team at Rockport, along with Massachusetts State Police Instructor Detective Michael Barrett. Now, four state police detectives were on the Johnson case. Assistant DA John Wilson arrived in Rockport to relieve Charles Green, who had been working nonstop since November 1.

The *Boston Globe* ran an article that touched on the emotions in Rockport:

> *These most recent developments have brought the inhabitants of this town to a state bordering on terror. The idea that a desperate and ruthless murderer is still at large in the community is raising havoc with the peace of mind of the population. The womenfolk complain that they cannot sleep anymore and the menfolk are wearing worried looks on their faces. The pressure on the Rockport Selectmen has been so great that they appealed today to the district attorney to do everything possible to push the investigation.*[59]

Aware of the citizens' perceptions, Assistant DA Wilson, Detective Griffin, Rockport Selectmen Chair Ralph Parker and Police Chief Sullivan met in a closed-door conference. They decided to put into action a mobilization plan the district attorney had recommended. The district attorney then made a phone call to General Daniel Needham, commander of the Massachusetts State Police.

That evening, the SCC hosted gospel preacher/singer Uncle Elmer and His Merry Musicians at a fundraiser for the Ladies Aid Society. Uncle Elmer was a popular entertainer who sang on the radio station WHDH on Sunday mornings. The church was packed with an estimated 250 people. Mrs. Albert M. Johanson was emcee and played the organ. Elmer and his choir sang old-fashioned gospel favorites. The SCC choir sang "Hallelujah for the Cross," and Ms. Eunice Johnson gave a solo performance of the ever-popular hymn "Someday We'll Understand." Warren Olson and the reverend's son Bernard passed the collection plate. The reverend closed the meeting with a benediction. State police troopers sat in the front pew, heads turned to watch the audience. After the concert, they walked home anyone who wanted an escort.

The Rockport Selectmen issued a statement:

> *The Board of Selectmen would inform the citizens at this time that all possible will be done to carry to a successful conclusion the operation of the apprehension of the murderer of Mrs. Augusta Johnson, and we hope that the people of the town will not be over-excited about the matter.*
>
> *A meeting called by the Board of Selectmen yesterday afternoon with District Attorney Cregg, Mr. Lane and Mr. Parker being present, this situation was thoroughly considered. Mr. Cregg was asked by Mr. Lane and Mr. Parker to offer the extra $1,000 reward as had been previously suggested by the Essex County Commission. Mr. Cregg informed the board that he intended to increase the force by at least four more men and comb the town thoroughly. Mr. Cregg also informed the board that he would cooperate in every possible way, and requested the aid of every person that can offer any suggestion to help find the solution of the case. As there are no very definite clues, the work is much more complicated and requires all aid that can be given.*[60]

This statement was only the beginning.

That night, as Uncle Elmer sang and people crowded into church, ten additional state troopers arrived in Rockport. From the Topsfield Barracks came William Faron, Francis Byrne and Daniel Jacobs, a Gloucester man on his first assignment. He had recently married his Rockport sweetheart Eunice Tucker and had just come back from his honeymoon. From the Foxboro Barracks came James Ready, William Moran and Daniel Hannigan. From the Reading Barracks came Trooper Arthur Chaisson, a former coast guard sailor who served in a cutter on Prohibition patrols. From the Concord Barracks came Norman Sidney. From the Framingham headquarters came Arthur Skillings. Finally came trooper James Donahue. The troopers would spend the night in Rockport, some at the Rockport Fire Station, sleeping on cots donated by the town fire department and the local chapter of the American Legion. Others were to sleep in the homes of private citizens in Pigeon Cove, houses in which residents feared that their lives were in danger.

That night's ten troopers were just the first wave of an invasion. More than thirty-five state troopers would be assigned to the Johnson case, a contingent that would work eighteen-hour days, with a reserve unit always on call. They would conduct house-sweeps by day and patrol the dark streets at night. In interviews, they would use a standardized form with the following questions:

- Do you know anything that would help us find the murderer of Mrs. Johnson?
- Where were you and what were you doing during the early morning of the day she was killed?
- Have you any well-founded suspicions that would help us?
- Has any food been stolen from your house recently?
- Did you see any suspicious looking persons around Rockport immediately preceding the murder?

The state police would search all 1,200 structures in Rockport and interview every adult resident, roughly three thousand people. Lobsterman or stonecutter, bohemian artist or wealthy bank president, everyone was asked where they were on Halloween night. It was an unprecedented push for information from an entire population.

The detectives were confident that the two murders were committed by the same Rockport resident. They were desperate to apprehend the killer. This was the plan to break that stalemate and make an arrest. The Johnson investigation—the search of one thousand homes, the demand for three thousand alibis—would be national news.

The manhunt began on November 9.

19

THE MANHUNT

Multiple newspapers covered this new phase of the investigation. It was as if the Fourth Amendment had been repealed. No warrants were needed, no cause needed to be shown. Everybody's constitutional rights were waived by public acclaim or per decision of the selectmen. *Boston Globe* correspondent Geoffrey Parsons Jr. commented, "For the time being, the inhabitants are throwing overboard their rights to resist a search of their homes without due process of law." The *Boston Post*'s Edwin B. Inglis wrote, "Tonight one of the grimmest steps ever taken by any police force in America was revealed—the turning inside out of every one of one-thousand homes for evidence." The *Boston Herald* described it as "one of the most sensational man-hunts in the history of the Commonwealth." The *Boston Globe* called it "a drastic and unprecedented police measure…to assist in one of the most thoroughgoing investigations ever made into an exceedingly puzzling murder mystery." Out-of-state papers ran the AP wire story on the plan, which it called "the most concentrated and unique hunt for a criminal in the history of police investigation in Massachusetts."

So, it was a very big deal.

The *Gloucester Daily Times*, perhaps perturbed at the presence of so many "metropolitan dailies" on its home turf, had a more skeptical take on the pantry prowler ("the thefts were more in the nature of foraging, a practice as old as the well-known hills") and had this to say about the search:

> The terror that grips the townspeople, especially the womenfolk, would seem to be without reason, but to allay their fears, the district attorney

Rockport and state police officers conduct a house search. *From the* Boston Daily Record.

has brought every state trooper available to the town, while three special officers have been appointed by the selectmen to join the regular patrolmen. Volunteers have also come forward to be on the lookout for any suspicious actions or circumstances. That people are apt to "see things" under such circumstances as the present is certain, and in the meantime, the men-folk are acting as guards of their homes, staying by the fireside. However, it is a mighty serious matter which every townsman, from the selectmen down to the laborer, all of whom are eager to do their part in apprehending the fiend.[61]

In part, in the hysteria, nobody wanted to risk their neighbors' suspicions by seeking to protect their homes from the invasion of the boys in blue. What have you got to hide? This would have been the next question posed to any Rockporter who brazenly chose to not allow searchers to step into their parlors, kitchens and bedrooms. Everybody cooperated. Nobody counted the number of Rockport housewives who raced to clean their homes in advance of the troopers, not wanting to look shabby.

Thursday, November 9, 1933

The morning was icy cold when fifteen state police troopers, organized into teams of three, began the search. The teams started in the Sheep Pasture neighborhood first and then expanded the search to Pigeon Hill, then Pigeon Cove, downtown and finally the outlying summer houses, then closed for the winter. Police contacted caretakers for house keys. The troopers would not only question residents using the standardized form, but they would also search every home and structure along their route. At the day's end, troopers would return to town hall with their interview paperwork. State Detective Griffin compiled the paperwork. The DA and assistant DAs formed a triumvirate to weigh the evidence and decide on subsequent courses of action.

Massachusetts State Police Sergeant John Sullivan, in charge of coordinating the town search, met with Detective Griffin regarding the logistics of billeting the troopers in town hall. The auditorium on the second floor was designated as the sleeping area. The Framingham State Police Barracks provided twenty-two cots. There was only one sink on the second floor. Selectman Parker, a plumber by trade, offered to set up a temporary shower system. The selectmen arranged for a new wood stove for added heat. There was discussion on setting up some sort of state-sponsored commissary; to date, troopers had to purchase their meals out of their own pocket at local restaurants.

Assistant District Attorney John Wilson was in town hall. Detectives Barrett and Ferrari were away on errands. The DA himself arrived later in

Police, detectives and the Assistant DA reviewing the standardized questionnaire. *From the Boston American.*

the day. Downstairs, the town clerk fielded more firearms licenses. A dozen more Rockporters had applied for permits that week.

There was news of Rudolph Ranta. His brother showed reporters a letter from Rudolph, postmarked from Paris, Maine. Aware that the police were looking for him, Rudolph was on his way home. The brother did not explain how Rudolph ended up north or why he went there.

Two days before Ada's murder, retired quarryman Jacob Keisala of 6 Oakland Avenue reported the theft of a hammer. One day before the murder, someone reported a quarryman's shack had been broken into. Gloucester Detectives Burgess and Moody and State Trooper James Ruddy, accompanied by *Boston Globe* reporter Edward Kelley, found a hammer at the shack crime scene. It wasn't Keisala's hammer or the murder weapon. Someone else brought into town hall a different rusty hammer, rounded on both ends. The state police pronounced it was "just another hammer."

One by one, state troopers reported for duty at Rockport Town Hall after their morning court appearances. Massachusetts State Police Sergeant Toelken gave his official report to the investigation team.

It was a problematic crime scene, with many smeared or otherwise unidentifiable clues. There were two conclusively identifiable prints. One of Ada Johnson's fingerprints was found on the Milk of Magnesia bottle. On the wooden ledge of the pantry window were the right-hand fingerprints of Warren Olson. No other prints could be identified. Toelken posited that the killer could have worn gloves or perhaps never touched many surfaces.

By nightfall, all teams had returned, and a night patrol set out to walk the streets in Pigeon Cove.

No one refused a search of their premises, and there were no incidents of noncooperation. Given the day's progress, detectives projected that they could compete the townwide canvass sometime between November 12 and November 15. The *Boston Globe* now reported difficulty talking to residents ("It's almost as difficult to get into a Rockport house nowadays as it was to 'crash' a speak-easy in the early prohibition era.") but said that the townspeople felt safe having the state troopers around.

In a brief news conference, Detective Murray hinted at possible good news by Saturday, based on the offstage efforts by Detectives Barrett and Ferrari. Murray confided that investigators had no solid motive but had a theory they could not share. Investigators believed the Oker and Johnson murders were not just related but also premeditated and planned. They believed the killer chose the times of attack and had an exit strategy. They believed the murderer left the Oker store "by some other method" (i.e. presumably not the front door). They mentioned that an accomplice may have been used, "perhaps unwittingly." They were looking for this accomplice as well.

"We are doing everything humanly possible to solve this crime!" Cregg stated.

That evening, Emil Niskanen, age thirty-six, an unemployed Finn surviving off town welfare, had a bit to drink. He already had a reputation for bothering local girls in the neighborhood. A Pigeon Cove woman saw him weaving down the street and thought he was a prowler. When she screamed, her cries caught the attention of two newspaper photographers and a special policeman. The night-shift state troopers quickly arrived on the scene. Niskanen was too drunk to be questioned effectively, but he muttered something about Pigeon Hill. Detective Griffin ordered the troopers to arrest Niskanen for public drunkenness and take him to the Rockport Police Station. He could sober up in the solitary jail cell.

Niskanen lived in a henhouse on the Mattson farm near Ada Johnson's home. State Trooper Faron and Rockport Officer James Quinn searched his shack. Was Niskanen the pantry bandit? Nothing turned up. In jail, Niskanen complained that the beef stew he had just prepared back in his hut was going to waste. *Boston Globe* correspondent Geoffrey Parsons Jr. later wrote that Niskanen was "more the victim of unusual circumstances than of his own offenses against society."

Friday, November 10, 1933

In the morning, ten additional state troopers, several from the West Bridgewater Barracks, arrived in Rockport. They carried blankets and bedrolls for their assigned cot in the town hall auditorium. The investigation team was now composed of twenty-nine state troopers, four state detectives, the entire Rockport Police Department and two Gloucester Police detectives, plus the DA and his two assistants. More state police were expected to arrive over the weekend, swelling the number to fifty. Troopers from every state police barracks in Massachusetts were participating in the Johnson case. General Needham had come through for Cregg.

Selectman Parker finished setting up the temporary shower. Patrols went out on the door-to-door search. A team searched the Olson house on Oakland Avenue. At Gloucester District Court, Judge York sentenced Emil Niskanen to five months in the Salem House of Correction.

A clue came up during the first one hundred interviews during the house-to-house canvass. A neighbor of Ada Johnson's told state police officers that they saw a bundle of clothing floating in a quarry. Troopers began dragging the quarry. News articles did not specify which quarry it was, but the big ones near the Pigeon Hill neighborhood were Steel Derrick and Big Parker Pit, about one thousand feet to the south of Ada's home.

Another Agitated Clergyman

The Reverend Raymond Calkins, a summer resident of Cove Hill Lane and pastor of the Federated Church in Pigeon Cove, just down the street from the SCC, visited Rockport Town Hall in an agitated state. He demanded to speak to investigators. Detective Griffin complied.

Calkins asked if Griffin knew about the death of five-year-old Rockport boy Bertrant Tompkins Jr.

The boy was at his grandfather Eric Natti's house in Lanesville, about two miles from Ada Johnson's house, when he disappeared on the afternoon of September 28 while playing outside in the yard. It was strange that the boy left without his dog, a constant companion.

His family had been looking for the boy for an hour when Eric Natti received a telephone call. He picked up the receiver, and an unidentified man's voice said, "Have you found Bert?"

Mr. Natti replied, "Why, no, we haven't."

"Do you want to find him?"

"Certainly, we want to find him," Mr. Natti replied.

The phone line crackled and clicked. The unidentified caller hung up.

Later that evening, the boy was found floating in a nearby quarry. Accidental drowning was attributed as the cause of death, although no autopsy was performed. Calkins wasn't so sure the death was accidental.

Detective Griffin wasn't sure what to think.

After another informal discussion with SCC pastor Reverend Johanson, Griffin spent the rest of the afternoon reading seven hundred interview reports. Two days into the manhunt, the paperwork had piled up so much that the detective requested a state police stenographer to come to Rockport to set up some sort of filing system to handle it. The troopers were thorough in their house-to-house search—two hundred residences so far, plus barns and outbuildings. They made detailed notes of everything they saw. They went into every room in every building. They checked clothing in closets; one resident told a reporter that staties had checked the cuffs of his trousers and his shoes for blood.

The *Boston Evening American* wrote:

> *The house-to-house canvass and search, as audacious as it is unique, is a measure born as much of the desperation of the police as of the fears of the community.... It's bound to embarrass a lot of innocent persons who have either forgotten what they were doing the night Mrs. Johnson was killed, or consider it nobody's business but their own.*[62]

Prowlers at the Pastor's

Detectives Griffin, Ferrari, Barrett and Murray met in Gloucester to discuss the case over dinner in a private room at the Hotel Savoy. Journalists tailed them but could do no more than report the bare fact of a meeting. The team may have been going over that day's compilation of interview reports. The inspectors gave no official statement regarding what they discussed or what they ate.

That night in Rockport, no one walked the streets save for the state police patrols. Reverend Johanson and his wife and son were at their home at 177 Main Street, on the stretch of road that led to the boundary with Gloucester. Johanson had spent an hour that afternoon with Detectives Barrett and Griffin, discussing the case. This is what the reverend told the *Boston Traveler* about what happened next:

> *My wife and my son and myself were seated in the living room following dinner. Mrs Johanson heard the machine drive up outside the home, and while this would in ordinary times go unnoticed, every noise of a machine or anything else, stands investigation.*
>
> *My wife went to the window. She saw two men get out of their machine and she summoned me and my son Bernard to the window. Peering through the windows, we saw the two men try the front door of the house. They looked suspicious from the beginning. There was a light in the window of the house, but the men were refused admittance. We saw the light go out in the parlor.*
>
> *The two men then ran down the front steps and went to the rear of the house. When I saw this, I immediately put on my hat and coat, for it was*

cold, and my son, who is a football player at Rockport High School, ran over across to the house. But apparently the men saw us coming and before we could reach the house the pair got into the machine.

It was dark but we both saw the men. The lights of the machine were turned off and the tail-light was all turned off, unabling us to see the registration.

They were bad looking men. If they were there for any good reason they would not have run away like that. After I had made known my identity, the two women who occupy the house all alone opened the door. They were so frightened they could not speak.[63]

Other newspapers clarified and possibly embellished the story. A likely clarification was that the prowlers mistakenly approached the house next door and then trespassed onto the Johnson property, where they walked toward the back door and then alongside the house to the front door. The perhaps embellished part was the account that the reverend, clutching a double-barreled shotgun, flung open the front door. Seeing a man of the cloth armed with St. Paul's "sword of the spirit" and the blue steel of Remington Arms in tandem, the prowlers fled.

Mrs. Johanson called the Rockport Police. She reported prowlers to Officer Spates, who was on desk duty at the time. Spates must have alerted Chief Sullivan, because Sullivan called the Gloucester Police to ask them to seal the Blynman Bridge and send units to the Gloucester-Rockport line.

Chief Sullivan did not call town hall, where up to fifty state troopers were billeted, a straight shot half a mile away from the Johanson house. Instead, the chief and four Rockport officers sped to the town border, a straight line down about a mile and a half south of the Johanson house. Gloucester Sergeant David Mehlman Jr. sent all available units—three police cruisers—to the city border. The Gloucester Police set up a roadblock at the Blynman Bridge.

The message to the Gloucester Police got garbled in translation, a real-world game of telephone. Instead of looking for a brown coupe, the Gloucester Police looked for a truck. The police stopped a truck driven by John Niskanen, forty-two, and passenger Johannes A. Oman, twenty-two, both from Pigeon Cove. John was the cousin of Emil Niskanen, who had just been arrested for drunkenness and had his henhouse hut searched. They detained Niskanen and Oman and sent them to the Rockport Police Station, where the men were briefly questioned and released.

Chief Sullivan met with Gloucester Police at the town line. By this point, the Gloucester Police had gotten the correct information on the vehicle type.

The police may have stopped multiple vehicles, but none of the Cape Ann police spotted a tan coupe, the preferred car of local murder suspects.

Two hours after Mrs. Johanson's phone call, Detectives Barrett and Ferrari walked into the Rockport Police Station and heard the news of the prowler and the local police search. They immediately sent two squads of Massachusetts State Troopers to the Johnson house.

The Gloucester, Rockport and Massachusetts State Police continued looking for the vehicle with its suspicious occupants. They looked all night. They never found it.

The *Boston Traveler* reported:

> *Whether it was just an oversight on the part of the local police could not be learned but the incident caused much discussion among state investigators, who deplored the lack of co-operation today. It was felt that unless all police agencies co-operate in the apprehension of this fiend, who has brought terror to the townsfolk, the work of the police will be of no avail.*[64]

Saturday, November 11, 1933

On another freezing cold day, two dozen state troopers continued the house-to-house canvassing. The *Globe* likened the process to looking for a needle in a haystack. The investigators would dismantle the haystack, straw by straw, until the needle was found. Because several local granite cutters left town to work in a quarry in Chelmsford, their wives stuck together in groups for mutual protection. Despite the presence of so many staties, no progress had been made. Residents were depressed and angry.

The *Boston Traveler* printed one young Rockport man's response to the manhunt:

> *Gave them all the information I possibly could and they asked me if I would take them through the house. I did this gladly, but when they looked at my suits in the closet, picked up my shoes and nosed into things which I thought rather personal, I kind of felt they were going too far.*
>
> *Although I didn't say anything, they apparently saw the look of anger on my face, for one trooper explained the necessity of such a search. They explained that unless I was willing to allow them to conduct the search the*

Police interrogate an Oakland Avenue resident. *From the* Boston Post.

way that they wanted, they would have to post a trooper at my door while another went back to town hall for a search warrant which would entitle them to search as they pleased.[65]

News of prowlers at the Johansons' house had a big impact. Clearly, the reverend was no random victim. All knew that the Revered Johanson had been questioned multiple times and cooperated with the investigators. Perhaps the prowlers were attempting to intimidate the Johansons to get them to go silent. The news from the *Boston Globe* of the lack of coordination between the state and Rockport Police the previous Friday night indicated poor communications at best and hinted at some deeper rift. Police on Cape Ann were still searching for the tan coupe, which they speculated had not left Cape Ann. But the coupe seemed as spectral as the war party of French and Native raiders reported in Gloucester during the 1692 witch hysteria. The DA met with Chief Sullivan to discuss the matter and improve communications across the departments involved in the case.

Speaking of improving communications, the *Boston Traveler* reported friction between the Gloucester inspectors and the state police. Gloucester Officers Moody and Burgess typically worked as a team. State Detective Griffin wanted to separate them. In response, Burgess and Moody threatened to quit. Griffin worked out a compromise: the two investigators could continue to work together but with a state trooper assigned to them.

Two "alienists" (i.e. psychologists) arrived in town to question Rockport residents. Their identity was secret. According to journalist William Brawthers of the *Boston Daily Record*, their assignment was to "mingle quietly with the townsfolk," and he said, "If they come across any individuals who show symptoms of a type of insanity which might cause such crimes as the killing of Mrs. Johnson and Arthur F. Oker…that individual will be subject to severe grilling." It is unclear how these two undercover shrinks worked with the investigation team or whether they found any valuable leads or symptoms of insanity.

In the afternoon, Detective Ferrari found Ada's wedding ring in the remnants of the burnt mattress in her backyard. The *Boston Daily Record* reported that if this state police canvass attempt did not work, Cregg was open to calling in troops to surround the area. Ada Johnson's house, of course, would be at the center of that circle.

Sunday, November 12, 1933

The bitterly cold morning saw a dusting of snow. Forty state troopers were in Rockport. Fifteen troopers under the command of Lieutenant Thomas Mitchell formed a cordon around the Pigeon Cove neighborhood. No one was permitted in or out of the area while the policemen went from house to house conducting interviews with the residents and searches of their property. If a person's alibi for Halloween night seemed odd or suspicious, the troopers were instructed to flag that resident for later escort to town hall for questioning by the assistant DA and the state detectives. Anyone who refused the house search would have their name turned over to the district attorney. Eighteen Pigeon Cove residents could not adequately describe what they were doing on Halloween. At the SCC, Reverend Johanson gave a sermon titled "Sign of the Times."

Hundreds of cars drove through Pigeon Cove and down Pigeon Hill Street and Oakland Avenue. There was a traffic jam, as so many people wanted a glimpse of what was now being called "the murder house." Some folks parked, got out of their autos and walked across Ada Johnson's snow-covered yard. They pressed their faces to the cold windows to look at the darkness inside.

Dream Girl, Hub Cop

At 3:30 p.m., Warren Olson was in his yard talking to some friends. A couple state police troopers were patrolling the area. An automobile drove up—the neighborhood had been inundated with drive-by gawkers all afternoon—but this automobile stopped in front of Warren's house.

A blonde woman of medium height got out of the car along with a man in civilian clothes. They approached Warren. The woman said she was from Quincy, the wife of a Boston policeman, presumably the man with her. She needed to talk to Warren right away.

She had a dream the previous night—no, not a dream, a communication from a saint. The saint told her that if she went to a house across the street from the Johnson house, she would find a key to a cave in the woods five hundred yards from the house, where there would be a clue to the murder. She felt a sense of urgency. Was the cave a hideout? Could the murderer be there now?

The important thing was that Warren was that key.

While she was talking, the man said something to a nearby state trooper. He turned back to his wife and Warren. "Let's go," the man said.

Warren didn't want to go.

The *Boston Daily Record* later reported that Warren was "dragged" to the car; perhaps that is a bit of gumshoe hyperbole. Perhaps it was nothing more than the man's firm grip on Warren's elbow. There was possibly another man in the car in a police uniform. Perhaps he got out of the vehicle to encourage Warren to get in. The uniformed man declined to show his badge or any sort of identification. It is unknown if he was armed.

Warren got into the car.

The quartet drove a short distance into the Rockport woods, following her directions, to a grout deposit. The husband-and-wife dream team talked to Warren. At first, the conversation was very woo-woo. The pair questioned Warren at length about Ada Johnson, so much so that he got suspicious. He clammed up.

They dropped Warren off back at his house two hours later, leaving him in the dark.

The Policeman in the Pulpit

What happened at the Swedish Congregational Church that evening was extraordinary. It was a singular event in the history of Massachusetts. The Massachusetts State Police had never done anything like it, nor would they ever do it again.

The congregation assembled in the church, with journalists crowding the back pews. It was quiet. Everyone was silent until Reverend Johanson spoke. When the pastor reached the pulpit, he made a surprise announcement. He told them to expect momentarily "your pastor for tonight." Then he sat down.

Two state troopers dramatically entered the church from the main door in the rear. Trooper Searles positioned himself by the door while Trooper Ernest Thorsell strode confidently down the center aisle toward the pulpit. Vestments covered Thorsell's "French and electric blue" uniform. As he walked up the aisle, congregants caught a glimpse of handcuffs and Thorsell's regulation .45-caliber service pistol at the sides of his black clerical fabric.

Tall, straight-backed and with a thick head of tousled blond hair, the twenty-seven-year-old Ernest Thorsell was based at the Framingham Barracks. He had been on the force for only two weeks. This was his first assignment. He was pastor of the Union Church in Foxboro and spoke fluent Swedish. Hearing of Thorsell's unique qualifications, DA Cregg asked the new trooper to speak at the SCC. Thorsell and Detective Griffin had discussed the details with Reverend Johanson over lunch earlier in the day, and together, they hatched the plan for Thorsell to conduct the sermon.

Thorsell introduced himself and said the following:

> *I don't believe that the murderer of Mrs. Augusta Johnson two weeks ago and Arthur F. Oker, eighteen months ago, sits in this congregation....But what may be true is that some member of this congregation has information which he or she is afraid to disclose. If you have any information about these crimes, it is your duty and obligation to disclose it. I urge you to come to me, both as a policeman and a minister of the gospel and tell me anything you know....Wherever the murderer is, I appeal to him to unload the guilt from his conscience. Unless he confesses his crime in this life, then for him there will be no afterlife....I assure you in the strictest privacy if you come to me, and I will pray for you as a brother in Christ, until you clear your soul. I will stay here all night, or all week, if you want me to.*[66]

Reverend Johnson kept his head bowed. Thorsell added, "When a police officer meets another, he is his brother in the law. When we have accepted Christ, we meet as brothers in love." He then asked the congregation, "How many of you want to walk with Christ?"

The congregants raised their hands.

Thorsell pointed to a congregant, saying, "Come to Christ with your confession of sin." He pointed to another congregant and repeated the phrase. And so on. Thorsell continued for thirty minutes, pleading with the congregants, "I will help you," and reminding the assembled that "there is an afterlife for you if you are free from sin." At his conclusion, Thorsell fired up the crowd, shouting, "Do you wish to walk with Christ?! Do you wish to walk with Christ?!"

One can imagine the reverent choruses of "Amens," the congregants, cheeks tear-stained, swaying and waving their hands in testament.

Reverend Johanson briefly preached in Swedish and attempted to announce the concluding hymn. Thorsell cut him off. He had a message specifically for the youth in the crowd: "You young folks have made no mistake in accepting Christ," he assured them. He then ordered Trooper Searles to escort the newspapermen out. Thorsell was going to pray along with the church youth group. He added, "I'll stay here tonight as long as you wish to have me. I'll stay through the week if you want me to."

Thorsell stayed in the church, praying with the kids. Searles guarded the door. After an hour, Thorsell dismissed the group. Thorsell took off his vestments. Thorsell and Searles headed to town hall to file their police report.

Newspapers wouldn't report it until later, but a congregant confided in Thorsell. Finally, just this once, someone in Rockport said something. They told Thorsell that Ada knew, or suspected, the identity of Oker's killer. She was murdered to keep her silent.[67]

Monday, November 13, 1933

Rockport jeweler Joseph W. Thibeault loaned the troopers a radio to help them pass the time when off duty. The troopers also had not one but three pianos to play, but only two troopers knew how to play the piano.

General Daniel C. Needham, the commissioner of public safety and head of the Massachusetts State Police, inspected the Rockport Town Hall billet to check on the troopers' accommodations. Needham spent three hours in Rockport, meeting with the investigative team before returning to Boston. He pronounced himself satisfied with the troopers' quarters and with the cooperation of the Rockport citizens, but he made no comment on the investigation or the murder. While in town, Needham, a dozen state troopers, four state police detectives, two Gloucester police detectives and the Rockport Police officers posed for the "moving picture cameras."

The Rockport Selectmen met with the district attorney and detectives. The board pronounced themselves satisfied with the efforts of the investigation team. Chairman Parker stated:

> *The State Troopers have conducted themselves everywhere like gentlemen. They have made a splendid impression on the town by the thorough, yet polite manner in which they are making their intensive investigation. We have no complaint to make whatsoever, although we would naturally like to see the murderer caught as soon as possible.*[68]

Detectives mentioned to the press that they were searching for a well-dressed man who stepped out from the woods between Gloucester and Rockport. The man came out of the woods at 1:30 (press reports garbled the time, some writing that the event occurred in the morning, while others stated it occurred in the afternoon) on November 1, and he attempted to hail a ride from a car transporting several young men from Beverly. The youths opted not to pick the man up, since he seemed sketchy. Detectives asked that the man come forward. They asked that anyone who might know this man or might have given him a ride to step forward.

The DA stated that he expected to announce results of Dr. McGrath's research on the following day. Griffin and Murray mentioned that the townwide search gave them more context to the Johnson case. They confirmed the rumor that Mrs. Johnson knew the identity of Oker's killer and was beaten to death to keep her quiet. They said that they had no definite proof but were investigating the allegation. They still believed that the murder was premeditated and that any robbery was an afterthought. Detective Griffin stressed that the killer was no maniac, that Rockporters were safe and that the state police would continue patrolling the town at night by patrol car and on foot. To date, four hundred homes had been searched, plus an unspecified number of empty and commercial buildings.

The *Gloucester Daily Times*'s coverage was pointedly at odds with the "the metropolitan dailies," which described the search as "irregular and even futile." Regarding the pastor's prowlers, the article stated:

It is unfortunate that any reference should have been publicly made as to rumored lack of cooperation between the local and state police since it is grossly untrue. The investigation is under the direct supervision of the district attorney's office, and thus far everyone has respected his right to map out the program of investigation, confident that only one skipper should be at the wheel.[69]

The image of a terrified town was incorrect, the *Times* added:

The majority of the people of Rockport are not as terrified as has been reported. They do get a distinctive thrill in having so much made of their small community, and the fact that 25 sturdy state troopers are within their boundaries making personal calls on them. They admire the efforts of the district attorney and his staff in trying to apprehend the guilty party. But the most of them have no fear that any one of them will be elected as the next victim, nor do most of them feel that there will be a "next victim."

The *Times* asserted that authorities believed that the "full-moon theory" and the "dream girl's" stories were bunk. But all papers had news to report about Warren Olson.

Warren Lawyers Up

Multiple newspapers, including the *Boston Globe*, the *Boston Daily Record*, the *Lynn Daily Item* and the *Gloucester Daily Times*, ran articles on Warren Olson. They described him as a former Lynn schoolboy, Sunday school teacher and grocery clerk. They described him as "chief witness" and "most helpful of any of the Rockport citizens connected with the case" who discovered Ada's battered body.

They also described him as livid over Sunday's "dream girl" incident.

Warren accused the investigators of a setup—they arranged his "kidnapping" in collusion with the state police and got a Boston Police officer to do the "dirty work." Warren stated, "They were talking to the troopers, and it was all a subterfuge to question me. There is nothing I am concerned about, and I have nothing to worry over."

Now Warren had a spokesman, Frederick Tarr Sr., Esquire. Mr. Tarr was not only the father of Rockport Town Counsel Frederick Tarr Jr., but he was also a graduate of Amherst College and Harvard Law School. He was a Royal Arch Mason and a member of the Cape Ann Oddfellows and Rockport Golf Club. He was a trustee of the Cape Ann Savings Bank, president of the Rockport National Bank and Gloucester Bar Association and chair of the Essex County Republican Club. An expert in maritime law and fishing rights, he was a former state representative and elected governor's councilor. He had served as U.S. attorney for Massachusetts and had just retired from the bench on the superior court.

Warren could not have selected a more prominent spokesperson.

Tarr said that Olson was just upset by the way he was "pestered by every Tom, Dick and Harry." Warren was happy to work with the authorities, he added, but not in this underhanded way. Tarr had just been asked to convey the message to the DA. When asked by a *Gloucester Daily Times* reporter if Warren was his client, Tarr snapped, "That's none of your business."

The press asked the Olson family if Tarr was Warren's attorney. August Olson told the press, "Warren doesn't want to answer any further questions." The family would not answer any questions from the newspapers either. August Olson did say that the Olson family would no longer cooperate with police until the state police gave some explanation for the kidnapping of Warren.

When DA Cregg got word of Tarr's involvement with Warren, Cregg denied that he had orchestrated an entrapment setup. He told the press that Warren had been interviewed so often because he had been such a helpful witness. Cregg didn't think Warren had ever been treated unfairly by the state detectives.

Detective Griffin was livid at Olson's suggestion that the investigators organized the Dream Girl and Hub Cop to surreptitiously question Warren. He described Warren as a valuable witness and expressed outrage that "unauthorized persons" would question or possibly attempt to intimidate him. He assumed it was just civilians playacting, eager for the selectmen's reward. He would reach out to the Boston Police Department about the matter. This was the third report to feature a psychic or a "dream-girl" proclaiming some sort of supernatural knowledge. This incident that neighbors were calling "an abusive outrage" was a silly distraction from the real investigation.

On November 14, DA Cregg and Frederick Tarr Sr. met. Afterward, Tarr told reporters that Cregg assured him he would issue orders to the police to use discretion in the manner of questioning Warren Olson.

The investigators never questioned Warren Olson again.

Tuesday, November 14, 1933

A bitter cold snap continued over Massachusetts. In Salem, attorney Sumner W. Wheeler filed a petition in district court, seeking to be appointed administrator of Ada Johnson's estate.

The *Gloucester Daily Times* devoted part of the day's Oker-Johnson coverage to Dr. William J. Hickson, a summer resident of Marble Street in East Gloucester. Dr. Hickson had a doctorate in philosophy from Switzerland and studied Gestalt psychology in Berlin. He was the staff psychoanalyst of the Chicago Municipal Courts for sixteen years. He and his wife often provided expertise on a freelance basis for criminal cases.

> *Many believe that Dr. Hickson would be especially valuable in the investigation of the two murders, for they are of the opinion that a psychoanalyst alone will be able to get to the bottom of the atrocities, since the murderer is apparently a mental case, and since there seems to be an absolute absence of facts, according to the admissions from the district attorney's office.*[70]

When the *Gloucester Daily Times* reporter called their summer home, Mrs. Hickson commented:

> *When asked as to whether she thought it inconceivable that a high mentality such as is accredited to the Swedish people as a whole, would be possible to murder in such a brutal manner, and whether it was not possible that an inferior type of nationality was responsible, she argued that nationality evidently has nothing to do with the matter, and that emotionalism of the subject alone could explain the real reason.*

Dr. Hickson was not available to consult on the case.[71]

The Junior Detective Corps

By mid-November, Cape Ann grocery stores had run out of breakfast cereal. The case of the missing Post Toasties was more solvable than the murders. Post Foods was running an advertising campaign aimed at children featuring Inspector Post and his Junior Detective Corps. So many Rockport kids mailed in the obligatory two box tops to Battle Creek for the shiny Junior Detective

Corps metal badge that they caused a run on the breakfast market. Packs of badge-wearing Rockport kids followed the state police as they conducted their house-to-house search, embarrassing the grown-ups.[72]

Toivo's Terrible Tour

At 8:00 a.m., Gloucester motorcycle officers George O'Maley and Albert Noble responded to a report of four suspicious men in a car parked at the base of the Gloucester Fishermen's Memorial statue on Stacy Boulevard. The officers found the men sound asleep in their sedan and arrested them. Toivo E. Huttunen (twenty-four), Walter Lasko (nineteen), Raymond Delaney (twenty) and Robert Mattson (twenty-two) lived in Norwood. The Gloucester Police brought the posse of potential vagrants to the station.

When questioned, Toivo admitted that he was originally from Lanesville and that his brother John Huttunen lived on Curtis Street in Pigeon Cove. Another of the men said that he, too, was formerly of Gloucester, of Finnish ancestry and that he also had relatives on Curtis Street. Reporting the story, the *Gloucester Daily Times* took note of the "League of Nations" aspect of the four men—Finnish, Irish and Swedish. The police thought something else.

Gloucester Police called in Detectives Ferrari and Michael Barrett, who arrived and interrogated the men for ninety minutes. It came out that Toivo and his pals were at a Beano game the night before in South Norwood when they got the idea to travel to Rockport, check out the murdered woman's house and visit Toivo's brother. They drove all night. Heading home, they ran out of gas on Stacy Boulevard. With all the service stations closed and without any cash, the men decided to sleep in their car and panhandle funds in the morning. The reformed Beano gamblers had not figured on being arrested and becoming "persons of interest" in a double homicide case. After the detectives were satisfied, Gloucester Police released the men with a stern warning and sent them on their way, presumably with some gas money.

The Evening News Conference

The investigation team held their evening press conference. The DA assured reporters that the investigation would not close until the killer was caught.

He added:

> *This is the situation. We believe that the crime must have been committed by some member of the community. We have not got much more than that to start on. That means if we draw a circle around Rockport we probably will include the murderer....*
>
> *Our problem is to narrow this circle down to one or two individuals by the process of elimination. We have gone through half the town and have made definite progress, at least to the extent of eliminating a large number of persons, and of proving false or true a large number of leads, and rumors which have faced us at the beginning of the investigation.*
>
> *From now on the investigation should progress more rapidly. I think we can speed it up materially. When the canvass of the entire town is finished we will go back to individual or individuals who are still left within the restricted circle.*[73]

The investigators gave additional commentary to the press that the state police were halfway through the townwide search and interviews. They confirmed that Ada Johnson knew the identity of the Oker killer; the confirmation may have come via Preacher-Trooper Thorsell from a member of the SCC. Detective Griffin stated that he was confident the state police were not involved with the dream girl incident but stated that they might want to do another search of the Olson house. The most eye-opening news was the comment that the Rockport Police had told the state police that a similar fire attempt was found at the Oker crime scene. A pile of cloth had been set on fire in the corner of the tailor's shop back on May 21, 1932.

But the fire went out.

Wednesday, November 15, 1933

Midweek, there were two news reports that did not get the attention they deserved.

The *Boston Herald* reported that a mortgage foreclosure filed by a Rockport bank and registered in the Essex County Register of Deeds on November 15 may be a clue to the motive for the killing of Ada Johnson. The filed property foreclosure involved a Pigeon Cove family who had been under investigation. The tip had been given to Detective Murray. The working theory was that someone affiliated with this foreclosure went to Oker for financial assistance, was rebuffed and consequently killed him.[74]

The second news story covered an event in Groveland, a mill town on the Merrimack River, thirty-seven miles northeast. Motor vehicle inspectors Roy B. Chase and Charles A. Woods were driving to Haverhill when they saw a car whose license plate was attached with rope. They stopped and interrogated the driver, Charles B. Davis of Ipswich. The vehicle's plates belonged to Ida Oker, the widow of the slain Rockport tailor. Davis was apparently "uncertain as to some angles of the ownership of the car," and the inspectors took him to the Haverhill Police Station. Davis claimed that he had bought the car in Salem, but a quick check proved this incorrect. The auto had not been registered since 1930. Riding with Davis was Ipswich resident Hallett Doyle. Two full pint bottles of alcohol and ten empties were found in the car. Chase and Woods notified the state police, who contacted the Rockport Police.

The *Newburyport Daily News* covered the preceding story, which presents us an opportunity to cover rumrunning in Rockport.

Rockport's most famous citizen was temperance advocate Hannah Jumper, who, in 1856, led a band of local women on a raid against the local saloons and liquor distributors. Hannah commanded the distaff posse brandishing a hatchet. Her actions led to the town becoming dry for decades—at least nominally. But in Rockport, with its hard-drinking populations and location adjacent to the boozy port of Gloucester, the legality didn't match the reality. Depression-era Rockport was very wet.

Prohibition was the "noble experiment," intended to eradicate the vice of intoxication. It failed and resulted in a host of unintended consequences, one of which was smuggling, or "rumrunning." Despite a coast guard flotilla of seven patrol boats based in Gloucester, rumrunning was big on Cape Ann. Canadian ships filled with crates of alcohol would stop, immune from authority, just outside U.S. territorial waters. Smaller boats from all the seacoast North Shore towns would meet these mother ships, load contraband and sneak back to unload ashore.

The Rockport Police had their biggest liquor bust in January 1932, seizing four barrels and fifteen gallons of smuggled and home-brewed booze from a home on Gott Avenue. But even with such a relatively significant seizure remains the stubborn evidence that Prohibition in Rockport was more of a question of maintenance than complete eradication. The proverbial small fish got caught, while the big fish were allowed to get away.

Arthur Oker's grandson Roger Martin published two books of Rockport resident memories, including rumrunning anecdotes. There are accounts of booze stashed in the Mill Pond culvert and summer vacation homes and of fast speedboats making midnight errands. There are stories of residents reminding themselves to "mind their own business" when they heard truck motors and clanking bottles in the dark. There are even recollections of a telephone operator of a Main Street store being held at gunpoint while a boat unloaded on Front Beach. And then there's the time Chief Sullivan refused medical treatment to a couple of smugglers shot up in a firefight with the coast guard.[75]

It's unclear how Ida's car license plate ended up on a smuggler's car. Perhaps the plate was stolen. She probably knew nothing about it. But it's an odd incident, one that reinforces the fact that we can go only so far in understanding what 1930s Rockport was really like.

20

FAILURE

November 16–November 20, 1933

Thursday was bitterly cold, with temperatures in the teens. A state trooper patrol, guided by local resident John Peterson, looked for clues in the abandoned colonial village of Dogtown Common. They found nothing of value. The DA told journalists that he expected the troopers to complete their sweep of Rockport and interviews with all citizens by end of the following day. The staties would then return to their respective barracks. A small contingent of troopers would remain to support the Rockport Police.

Cregg explained that after the search was finished, there would be a conference of the entire investigation team, possibly as soon as tomorrow. Each member would share their thoughts and suspicions. They would go over all the interview materials. In reviewing the material, the team would determine if they had enough evidence to arrest someone. The DA mentioned there was a short list of persons of interest, but at this juncture, there was no physical evidence to link any of them to the crime scene.

The detectives scrutinized the fiscal health of Pigeon Cove residents, concentrating on individuals who personally knew and had monetary dealings with Ada Johnson and Arthur Oker. They wanted to know if anyone was in financial distress; perhaps that was a motive for murder. It was the Depression; there were many people in desperate financial straits—but not necessarily desperate enough to commit murder.

The detectives also focused their attention on another "prominent member" of the SCC. This was a person who "has never been mentioned prominently in the investigation" and came under recent suspicion due to the recent house-to-house search:

> *Adroit work on the part of the detectives has brought forth some startling contradictions from him and members of his family. They are startling in view of the facts given the troopers and the detectives by neighbors, facts which have been verified.... The grilling, police admitted tonight, will cause a sensation because of the fact that suspicion has been pointing elsewhere for days.*[76]

On Friday, the week-long cold snap broke, with the high temperature reaching twenty-five degrees Fahrenheit. News outlets reported that there was a new person of interest in the case, a member of the SCC who had known and had financial dealings with both Oker and Johnson. He would be questioned, and depending on how the session went, the DA stated that he would know within forty-eight hours if he had enough evidence to warrant an arrest.

In the afternoon, Rockport Officer Quinn and Trooper Byrne intercepted Carl Strandhal as he got off the train at the Rockport railroad station. Strandhal, a paint maker by trade, was the SCC church caretaker and former treasurer. He was on his way back from jury duty at the superior court in Salem when he was picked up by police. Byrne and Quinn took Strandhal to the police station instead of town hall since it was a more secure, private location away from prying eyes of residents and journalists. State Detectives Barrett, Ferrari and Griffin questioned Strandhal for an hour and twenty minutes. Patrolman Quinn then brought Strandhal home.

After the interrogation, Detective Griffin told journalists that Strandhal had no knowledge of the crimes, but they wanted to ask questions and refresh his memory regarding recent events in the Pigeon Cove area. Whatever Strandhal said, it did not lead to a break in the case, nor the possibility of an arrest. By the end of the day, state police units had searched 1,700 structures in Rockport.

On Saturday morning, investigators spent two hours in town hall sorting through the remaining state police interview files and notes. The canvassing of Rockport was complete. There were no new leads nor evidence.

With their search complete, the state police units planned their exit. After ten days, twenty troopers from the Concord, Foxboro and West Bridgewater stations packed up their gear and returned to their barracks. Seven troopers, including Pastor-Trooper Ernest Thorsell, would leave Rockport at the end of the day. Going forward, a state police car from the Topsfield Barracks would patrol the Pigeon Cove and Pigeon Hill neighborhoods at night. The *Gloucester Daily Times* reported:

> Despite the intensive work done by the detectives and troopers since the investigation began on November 1st, nothing definite appears to have been established in regards to identifying the fiend. The detectives entertain their suspicions as to who might be the guilty party, but nothing has developed to warrant an arrest.[77]

In the afternoon, DA Cregg held a press conference alongside Assistant DA Charles Green and State Detectives Barrett, Ferrari, Griffin and Murray. Cregg announced that the state police troops had completed their work and were no longer needed. Investigators admitted that the case was baffling, but Cregg swore that they would not give up. Detective Griffin stated:

> We are doing everything, in fact we have been doing everything that we can think of. We have checked every story, rumor, clew that has been brought to us, even some that we were sure were hopeless.…We have no motive. We have no weapon. There was no reason that we can discover for any person wishing to kill Mrs. Johnson. She didn't keep any money to speak of.…She had no intimate male friends. No one saw or heard anything.
>
> You people don't realize how dependent a detective is on luck in a case like this.

On Sunday, November 19, the *Boston Globe* ran a full-page spread with photographs and an article summarizing the case by Geoffrey Parsons Jr. Parson mentioned that Ada's diamond ring was still missing, that both murders were committed around a full moon and that only two fingerprints were found at the Johnson crime scene, belonging to the victim and the next-door neighbor Warren Olson. He described the house-to-house search as an extraordinary measure endorsed by the Rockport Selectmen and added that Rudolph Oker was now running the tailor shop. Parsons concluded:

> That's the situation as it stands today. The outlook is not too hopeful. There is no established connection between the Oker and Johnson murders. There may never be another similar murder in Rockport. But if you live in the

little town that subsists on Summer visitors, lobstering and the remnants of an ancient granite quarrying tradition, you are going to be on your guard.[78]

On November 20, only Detectives Murray and Griffin remained in Rockport. They checked out a report of a man acting furtively, walking near a quarry with a large parcel under his arm. They did not find the man. The detectives then took a trip to Danvers State Hospital to interview John Mackie of Pigeon Cove. Acting erratically a while back, Mackie had complained to Rockport Police that he couldn't sleep since the Oker murder. The murder haunted his dreams. Mackie wanted to give himself up, as he heard that authorities had connected him to the Johnson murder. Mackie got hysterical. Instead of getting arrested, Mackie got committed.

Hospital superintendent Dr. Bonner refused Griffin and Murray permission to interview the patient. Mackie was just not mentally competent to talk to authorities. The detectives left the hospital.

The following Monday, November 27, these last two state detectives packed up their files and left Rockport. The *Gloucester Daily Times* commented, "It looks very much as if the Johnson investigation has traveled the same path as did the Oker investigation, and that once more Rockport has an unsolved murder, the solution of which will go with the murderer to his grave."

Detective Griffin spoke to the Lions Club at the Hotel Savoy in Gloucester on January 16, 1934. He gave an update on the unsolved homicides:

Detective Griffin told the Lions that the Rockport cases were not dropped, nor ever would be. He said that there were very real mysteries in police work, and the only ones he was ever connected with were the Rockport murders. In both these cases, he said there was no evidence that anything had been taken away as far as the police knew, and there was nothing dropped at the scene of the crime by the murderer. In most cases there was usually some sort of lead, but in these cases there was not, although there was no telling what persistence might develop, for persistence was one of the most essential qualifications for a state detective....Regarding the Rockport cases, he said everything had been done that experience had taught them should be done but thus far without success.[79]

The investigation went cold until the following October.

21

THE HAMMER

October 1934

On Sunday afternoon, October 14, middle-schooler Waldemar Rundgren, thirteen, was about to play football with some buddies in a field on Pigeon Hill near Hillside Road. The kids needed to mark some goal posts for their pitch. Waldemar looked around. He saw that an empty, rickety old shed on the edge of the lot that was built on a fieldstone foundation.

The boy approached the barn, scouting for suitable stones. At the corner of the barn, there was a stone just the right size on the outer edge of the foundation, resting on a jumble of other rocks. Waldemar crouched down and removed it. He immediately saw that the rock was resting on two other rocks, forming a little niche. Inside the space was a thick stick. Curious, he picked it up.

It was the handle to a hammer. The handle was crude, made from a tree limb with bark still on it, possibly birch. The blackish-brown metal head was heavy, weighing almost five pounds. It looked like it had been outside for a while, exposed to the elements. Something was adhered to the face of the hammer, black stains and what looked like matted straw or human hair.

Waldemar's thoughts immediately went to the recent killings in town. Perhaps he had stumbled on the murder weapon. So, what did he do?

He went back to his friends with his new goal post rock and played football. He thought, in the convoluted way teen boys think, that if there was another murder, he'd check the spot, and if the hammer was missing, then he'd know it was the murder weapon.

But Waldemar did something else. After playing the game, he went home a quarter mile away and told his father about his find. His dad immediately asked to be taken to the spot next to the barn where the boy found the hammer. They went back to the spot. The hammer was still there. They took it, and that night, at 7:45 p.m., they showed it to Chief Sullivan at the station.

Either Chief Sullivan or Waldemar's father placed the hammer in a paper bag. Waldemar told Chief Sullivan how he found the hammer. The chief promised to show the tool to State Detective Murray when he stopped by on Tuesday. Murray was still technically the detective overseeing the Oker-Johnson case, but since it had gone colder than Atlantic waters, he visited town only once a week.

On Tuesday, October 16, Detective Murray stopped by the Rockport Police Station. Chief Sullivan pulled out the paper bag and showed Murray the excitable kid's find. "It's just a stonecutter's hammer," Sullivan said. "It's the second hammer that someone's brought to the station. In a town filled with boatyards and granite quarries, there are hundreds if not thousands like it all over. It's no big deal. Looks like there's straw on it."

Maybe this case wasn't so cold after all.

Detective Murray informed DA Cregg about the find. He thought that this might be the murder weapon, a real break in the case. Murray was convinced that the hammer was deliberately hidden. The detective wanted to send the hammer to a friend at MIT for chemical analysis to determine if the stains and hairs were of human origin. He wanted to run a photograph of the hammer in the newspapers to see if its owner could be identified, perhaps by a local blacksmith. Murray would keep the forger's mark a secret from the press to prevent false claims.

On October 18, Detectives William and Murray traveled to Rockport with photographers to take pictures of the hammer and the location of the find. Searching the shed, detectives discovered a glass bottle containing an ounce of what appeared to be flammable liquid and the rotting remnants of what appeared to be smeared newspaper pages. The hammer was then sent to MIT. Assistant DA Charles Green then announced the find and stated that the investigators would ask for the bodies of Oker and Johnson to be exhumed to determine if they had both been murdered by this instrument.

Newspapers broke the story on Friday, October 19. The *Gloucester Daily Times* reported that the Rockport Police denied the boy's last name was

Left: Detectives at the shed and a close-up of the hammer. *From the* Boston Traveler.

Below: Waldemar points to where he found the tool. *From the* Boston Daily Record.

"Irundgien," as incorrectly reported by the *Boston Post*, and added, "The name of the boy was not disclosed by the police, who said that the boy's father had an idea that it might be the weapon, and that tragedy would be visited upon his home by the murderer if he knew who had unearthed the first clue." However, the father apparently didn't have an issue with the *Boston Daily Record* publishing a captioned photograph of his boy pointing to the spot where he had found the rock. Perhaps he confidently assumed that local maniacs didn't read the metropolitan dallies.

The *Boston Traveler* incorrectly reported the property owner as John Peterson and said that he had been questioned during the townwide search.

This was impossible, as "John" (aka Andrew K. Peterson) had died back in January 1933, long before Ada's murder. Other papers described the property owner only as a "prominent citizen" and a "prominent Rockport churchman," which got closer to the mark.

Andrew K. Peterson was not a churchman. But his son and heir, Axel E. Peterson (aka A.E. Kokkonen), was. Axel Peterson graduated from Ironweed Theological Seminary and changed his last name to the more Finnish-sounding "Kokkonen." He was a resident of both Jersey City, New Jersey, and Pigeon Cove, where he helped found the Finnish Chorus and recently preached at the Finnish National Church on Granite Street. In a town as small as Rockport, Kokkonen likely knew both Oker and Johnson, but it is unclear why he was such a person of interest for both the state detective and Chief Sullivan. DA Cregg announced, "This man is a member of the same church league to which the two victims belonged, told us during the initial investigation that he never had a stone mason's hammer in his possession." This was an odd statement: Kokkonen belonged to a Finnish Lutheran denomination, not the Swedish Congregational. He was certainly quite religious but not a "religious maniac."

Between October 19 and October 23, state police detectives dismantled the wooden shed in the hayfield, hunting for more clues. They found nothing. They questioned a Rockport hardware dealer who sold a glass cutter several days before the Johnson murder, but they couldn't—or wouldn't—recall who made the purchase. Investigators noted that nobody came forward to claim they bought the cutter. Detective Murray questioned one new witness and five others who had previously submitted statements. The investigators searched the Peterson household on Hillside Drive while Kokkonen was away, but they found nothing. They walked back the assistant DA's statement regarding the exhumations of the bodies of Johnson and Oker when medical examiner Ira Hull pointed out that the blunt-edged hammer found in the foundations could not have made the linear cuts on the victims' skulls. The authorities did not release any test results from MIT, which perhaps indicated that any chemical analysis, if done, was inconclusive at best or proved the samples to not be human hair and blood.

DA Cregg, facing multiple complaints from residents on the investigation's slow progress, promised that he would do his best to speed up the proceedings. Chief Sullivan declared, "My men have been working night and day to solve the murders."

Reverend Kokkonen told the *Gloucester Daily Times* that, yes, the hammer belonged to his late father, a fact confirmed by quarryman Paavo Nevala of Stockholm Avenue. Nevala claimed that he had made the hammer with the applewood shaft for Peterson back in 1931. Both Nevala and Peterson used the hammer for a time, but it eventually got misplaced or lost. Neither man used it to commit a murder. Kokkonen had never used it either. As for the accelerant, the *Gloucester Daily Times* acerbically commented, "As for the so-called clue of the fuel oil bottle, it has been suggested that a little more probing might find even more oil in that they do burn things once in a while on the old homestead." Not to mention that the flammable liquid angle was weak, since the state fire inspector had pointed out that no liquid accelerant seemed to have been used to set Ada Johnson's bed alight.

The renewed press coverage raised a couple intriguing facts that had never been previously reported. The first was that an electric flat iron was missing from Ada's house after her attack. The second was a report of a conversation between quarryman and SCC trustee Charles Johnson and Adolph Johnson, Ada's husband, in late May 1932. Adolph was dying of quarryman's lung, but he was apparently well enough to carry on a conversation.

Charles asked Adolph, "Don't you think that the police should have gotten someone for the Oker killing?"

Adolph replied, "That is easy. They should know who to pick up for that job."

But Adolph died just a couple days later before he could reveal who that easy suspect was.[80]

The inspection of the hammer was almost the last public act of investigation. No state detective visited the following Tuesday, October 24. DA Cregg, campaigning for re-election with ballots cast in early November, had other appearances to make and other people to see.

22

A SLAUGHTER OF SWANS

November 1–November 9, 1934

At 8:30 a.m., Cape Ann plumber Lawrence Swan, thirty-two, of Curtis Street on Pigeon Hill noticed that the family pets—a sheep and flock of ducks—were missing from their backyard enclosure. The animals had been snug and secured the previous evening, Halloween night. Swan walked around the neighborhood to find them. He found the sheep.

He then called the police.

Officer James Quinn arrived at the Swan house to discover a distraught plumber standing guard outside of his house with a rifle. Swan led Quinn to a nearby wetland, where the family sheep's throat had been slit cleanly lengthwise from chin to neck. A chunk of flesh was missing from its left hindquarter. Another leg had been severed. Two hundred feet westward, Officer Quinn found a pile of feathers next to a little nub of maroon-colored organ. It was a duck's heart. Quinn then found three ducks. They were in a crippled, pitiful state, heads half-severed from their necks, as if they were deliberately maimed.

This did not look like an animal attack.

Swan had no idea why anyone would hold a grudge against him. The sheep belonged to his young Swedish wife, Karen. They had been married the previous year. The ducks belonged to their elderly housekeeper, Albertina Johnson. Karen and Albertina were related. Albertina was related to several people in the neighborhood. In fact, her daughter-in-law used to live a few doors down the street on Oakland Avenue. She had died the previous year on Halloween night—her name was Ada Johnson.

By Saturday, news of the animal mutilation had electrified Rockport and reignited a press frenzy. Chief Sullivan's first reaction was cautious, almost blasé, as he pointed out that there was no proof the slash at the sheep's throat was made by a knife or a guard dog, of which there were several in the neighborhood. He was strongly skeptical that the incident had anything to do with the unsolved double murders. Sullivan placed James Quinn in charge of the investigation, with Officer Conley assisting.

The press was not blasé. "Slaughter of Animals Linked to Slayings" was the headline in the *Boston Globe*, followed by "Sheep Killing Seen as Maniac's Work." The *Boston Sunday Advertiser* got the facts garbled but the spirit of the story right with its headline "Cattle Slaughter Seen as Clue to Rockport Maniac." Sullivan denied reports that he had posted an officer at the Swan house. Swan was reported to be doing his regular plumbing rounds, unconcerned about the affair. He was also reported to be guarding his house with that rifle, stating, "I will shoot any stranger that comes onto the property."

DA Cregg, Detective Murray and state troopers came to Rockport for another round of interviews with increasingly taciturn Pigeon Hill neighbors. Murray speculated that a "shrewd and cunning maniac" had some sort of grievance against the entire Johnson family. There were reports that Chief Sullivan had posted an officer to the Swan property. Pivoting, the chief gave a statement to the *Boston Globe*:

> This was no Halloween prank of boys. No normal person come to the age of understanding would commit such an atrocity on a dumb animal. Hatred, deep and deadly, is stamped indelibly on this act. To the conviction links the Oker and Augusta Johnson murders with this latest occurrence, a theory that someone intimate in the inner circles of this little colony on Pigeon Hill Road is a Dr. Jekyll and Mr. Hyde, who cleverly seeks his time and occasions and perhaps uses disguises. That he is surprisingly clever is evidenced by the fact that he has thus far baffled and thrown off the track the shrewdest trackers of criminals in this section.[81]

Swan speculated that the attack might have been a warning to his aunt. Authorities thought along the same lines. Albertina was extremely upset. When questioned, she burst into tears and said nothing.

On November 9, Rockport Officers Ralph Levie and Anthony Costa discovered another mutilated sheep with "strange marks" on its throat in the middle of Washington Street, near the corner of Centennial Avenue. The animal's owner was Joseph George, who ran a shop on Market Street. Police determined the animal had been killed by a dog.

23

AFTERSHOCKS

In February 1936, Rockport Police received a series of odd telephone calls. Late at night or early in the morning, someone would call. When a desk officer answered, the person would laugh maniacally and then hang up. The laughing man called at least a dozen times but stopped around February 28, when two false alarms were called in from fire boxes nos. 63 and 64 in Pigeon Cove. Box no. 63 was where Carne pulled the level to report the fire at the Johnson house. The calls could not be traced. Whoever pulled the false alarms could not be identified.

The Lanesville Prowler
September 2–September 24, 1936

Gloucester Police logged multiple reports of sexual assault in Lanesville. On the night of September 2, a seventy-year-old woman reported that a prowler assaulted her in her own backyard on Leverett Street. Her alcohol-soaked assailant grabbed her throat and demanded ten dollars. She grabbed a pole and chased him out of her yard. Later that evening, a young woman on nearby Emerald Street was attacked. She ran into her house and locked the door. The following Saturday, September 5, the assailant jumped another young woman at the corner of Emerald and Washington Streets. She managed to break free of her attacker and run home. The Gloucester paper described the attacker's score as "zero-zero."[82]

On September 23, 1936, the *Boston Post* reported:

> *A volcano of fury smoldered in the Lanesville section of this town tonight and, as the mutterings of irate townspeople concerning the attacks on four girls during the past few weeks grew louder, threatened to burst forth and cause renewed action in the murder cases of Mrs. August Johnson and Arthur F. Oker of Rockport.*[83]

Lanesville parents of the girls claimed that the attacker was a man questioned in connection with the Oker-Johnson killings. Although every male Rockporter was questioned during the 1932–33 investigations, the parents insisted the girls could make a positive identification.

The next day, the *Gloucester Daily Times* used words like *rumors* and *absurd* in response to what it described as the "latest metropolitan news outbursts." It reported that the women could not identify who sexually assaulted them.[84]

Gloucester Police put plainclothes police patrols in the area. They also put an officer in drag to walk the streets as a lure. The prowler did not take the bait. Detective Griffin checked in with Gloucester Police on the morning of September 24 and then returned to Salem with no action taken.

THE BOY IN THE ALLEY
MARCH 22–MARCH 25, 1938

Mrs. Patrick Evans found seven-year-old Robert Forsman lying unconscious in an alley half a block from Oker's old shop. Barely alive, the boy had suffered head trauma and was bleeding from the nose. His cap was missing. There were no bloodstains on the street. Little Robbie Forsman was transported to Addison Gilbert Hospital in critical condition and was placed on the "danger list." His family was notified. Given his wounds, doctors ruled out the possibility of the boy being hit by a motorist.

Perhaps a certain hammer-wielding assailant had struck again.

The front page of the next day's *Lowell Sun* ran with the headline "Rockport Murder Maniac Bludgeons Boy in Alley." The *Boston Post* published "Boy Beaten Left as Dead." Rockporters panicked. Chief Sullivan assigned extra police patrols downtown, with the orders to be on the lookout for strangers.

Robbie Forsman died on March 25 without regaining consciousness. By then, officials had pieced together the facts; they were less sensational if no less tragic. A five-year-old boy had seen Forsman playing on the fire escape on a building parallel to the alley on the morning of March 22. The boy then saw Forsman fall and hit the cement ground or a rock. The boy saw Forsman pick himself up, dazed but with only a bloody nose. Assuming Forsman was OK, the boy neglected to tell his parents of the incident. Shortly afterward, though, Forsman apparently collapsed and lay in the alley for six hours before he was discovered. An investigator named Donald Babcock found Forsman's hat under the fire escape and blood on a nearby rock.

Police closed the case.

The Man in the Window
June 14, 1938

Detective Griffin headed back to Rockport. Chief Sullivan had alerted him that a potential new witness in the Oker cold case had come forward. Sullivan heard about him from Officer Jacob Perkio, a Finnish American who was new to the Rockport Police force. Perkio, in turn, heard it from this witness's former employer. The witness at the end of this game of telephone was a fifty-seven-year-old unmarried, semi-employed Finnish quarryman named Jacob Hilso. Detective Griffin, Chief Sullivan and Officer Perkio brought Hilso into the station to give a statement.

Hilso told the officers that around 11:00 a.m. on May 21, 1932, he was walking with his friends Matt Hakala and Nestor Salo down Main Street from Bearskin Neck and on their way to the "woods" to spend the day playing cards. Hilso stated:

> *As I was walking by the Oker store I looked in and saw a man waving his arm as though he were striking some one. He was on the side of the counter, that was in the back of the store, nearest the street. As I looked in the store I just caught a glimpse of the man's face. I did not see Mr. Oker or any other person in the store. The man saw me. He caught my eye. I continued on my way. I did not consider that it was important....About a month later I did talk about it with Nestor Salo. I did not tell the police. I made a mistake once before by telling the police about a man who was innocent. The man whom I saw in Oker's store was about five feet, nine inches tall, slim, very light complexion and wore a soft, gray hat. About two years later, in*

Gloucester, at about eight o'clock at night, I was in Miller's Drug Store, in Gloucester. The drugstore is at the junction of East and Main Sts. A man was in there. When I went out, he followed me. He said to me, "Do you know anything about the Oker murder?" He followed me and asked me the same question three or four times. I had been drinking. It was the same man whom I say in Oker's store on the day that Mr. Oker was killed. I think that I could tell the man if I saw him again. I was afraid when he spoke to me in Gloucester.[85]

Detective Murray and Officer Perkio took Hilso to 77 Main Street. They asked Hilso to point out the window from which he saw the man who caught his eye. He pointed at the window of the front door.

Detectives Griffin and Murray could not locate Matt Hakala, who had supposedly relocated to Randolph, Massachusetts, but they tracked down Nestor Salo, who also gave a statement. Salo verified that he had walked down Main Street that morning six years ago with Hilso and Hakala. Salo confirmed that the trio passed Oker's store around 11:00 a.m. but stated that did not see Hilso look into the store window. Salo verified that Hilso told him a month after the murder about what he saw in Oker's store window but added, "I did not go to the police. I don't know why."

Officer Perkio told detectives that Hilso drank and got drunk but "was not a bum." Perkio did not tell the state detectives that Hilso was well-known to the Rockport Police force. Back on Christmas Day 1932, Hilso and two other Finnish quarrymen, John Pakkala and Moses Manninen, got so stinking drunk on "White Mule" up on "Squam Hill" that Pakkala's wife called the police. When Officer James Quinn arrived at the domestic disturbance and attempted to arrest the men, they responded violently. Hilso "decided to get rough so that the officer had to swing on him with the club to make him behave." Pakkala was given a suspended sentence, but Manninen and Hilso earned a ninety-day stint in the county jail for assaulting a police officer.[86]

Detectives weren't sure what to make of the account, noting that if Hilso did look into the store door window at 11:00 a.m., it was before Linder left and the postman arrived. If Hilso passed by later in the morning, he couldn't have looked in the door window, as multiple other witnesses noted that the shade was pulled down. Officer Perkio promised to work with Hilso to see if he could better identify the man who accosted him at the Gloucester drugstore. The lead, if it was one, fizzled out.

The Blaring Radio Murder
December 11, 1939

Tailor Jeremiah P. "Jerry" Sudbury, age sixty-four, was bludgeoned to death with a hammer or pipe in his second-floor office above the Emmet Club on Main Street on the town square in Woburn. He was seen alive at 9:00 a.m. by friend and butcher Arthur Leland. Sudbury was in good spirits but busy with a rush alteration, so Leland didn't stay long.

Sudbury was partially deaf and would play his radio at an elevated volume. But later that morning, his radio was blaring. At 10:00 a.m., office neighbor Jimmy Winn checked in on Sudbury. He tried the door and found it locked. At 11:00 a.m., other office neighbors used a key to get into the office. They found the blood-drenched tailor dead in a corner.

Only one street entrance and a single set of stairs led to the second floor and Sudbury's office. There was no rear exit. It was surmised the killer came in broad daylight, turned up the radio and then, with his sound camouflaged, robbed and violently killed Sudbury before leaving via the street. Although he must have been covered in his victim's blood, nobody saw him.

Jerry Sudbury had worked out of that office for forty years. He was popular, with friends and customers stopping by at all hours to chat or play cards. He was also known to place small bets on numbers pools, horse races and other lotteries. He had just made a "hit" for $100 a couple days before his death, but that did not seem sufficient motive for robbery and killing.

Detective Edward J. Sherlock studied the crime scene, conducted multiple interviews and even had the serrated dial of the radio dusted for fingerprints. Sherlock found no leads nor clues. The Middlesex DA picked up on similarities between the Sudbury and Oker cases. He contacted Essex County DA Cregg to discuss them. But it didn't matter; one unsolved case didn't solve the other.

The Sudbury case remains open today.[87]

24

ECHOES

In 1938, Rockport lobsterman Gor Svenson (a pseudonym) gave a frank perspective on the unsolved Full of the Moon murders:

> *One time [1932] someone kill Swede tailor feller over on Main Street, Rockport. Right in day-time too. Everyone say that Cregg he get murderer. They say that he could not put Jesse Costello in jail and everybody sore. He'd better catch these murder all right, or he lost job. But he don't catch murderer. And he don't lose job, too! Maybe, Gor, you could catch murderer. Maybe, you have some police, some money, you go around ask questions, write down what they say, maybe you find out, get a lot of money, maybe they make you G-man. I got pretty good guess who kill Swede, anyway, I think maybe Finn people do it. Finn people do not like Swede fellers. I know some Finn fellers they are all right. Some my friends they Finn fellers. But they do not like Swedes. Swedes bigger, smarter.*
>
> *The morning after the next Halloween [following the Oker murder] I come to maybe eleven o'clock when I sell my lobsters Howard Hodgkins that feller says Hey Gor, you hear what happen, somebody kill Swede woman down Pigeon Hill Street? Feller tell me all about it. Somebody goes in that Swede woman's house kill her set fire to house! That was fire alarm I hear out in harbor. Hey, we have a lot of noise after that. They get army down here, get whole American army. They come round every house, those soldiers and police too. Fellers come from newspapers, too. Every day all over papers, "Murder in Rockport!" Everybody say he know who did it.*

In papers it tells police ask questions.... They ask me questions too. Sure. They ask everybody in Rockport questions. They come right in house, look everywhere, say, "Who are you? Where were you that night? Who you think kill that woman, harr?" But they do not get feller that kill that woman.[88]

In September 1941, the *Boston Sunday Post* ran a story about local unsolved murders. Correspondent Charles Haven wrote the section on the Rockport Maniac killings, which became the origin of the rumor that Rockporters supposedly knew the identity of the killer but refused to tell. Haven interviewed Rockport Police Officer James Quinn, who stated, "I always believed that a break would someday come in these cases. They will never be closed as long as I live. Some day, someone will talk or the murderer will make a slip. I'll be around when that occurs." Haven also wrote, "You will hear that scores of persons know the solo perpetrator of both crimes; that they could name his name, if abject dread didn't still their tongues."

Sullivan kept his post as police chief after the Johnson case went cold and kept his reputation as a cantankerous, controversial town official. In 1940, the Rockport Selectmen voted for Sullivan to be police chief for life, but it was the same year the chief got into an argument with the Rockport civil defense committee chair. Relations between the chief and the selectmen declined as World War II progressed, beginning with a fight over a 10 percent salary increase at the 1942 Town Meeting. That same fall, Rockport debated adopting the Essex County pension system, which stipulated a mandatory retirement age. The octogenarian Sullivan refused to go, but in September 1943, the selectmen forced him out.

Upon retirement, Chief Sullivan completed one last bit of unfinished business. H. Lawrence Jodrey Jr. recalled:

And then there was your poor grandfather's murder (Arthur Oker, in 1932). I remember a picture down the police station one time and it showed blood all over the place. Another artifact was the pistol that a banker had blown his head off with. A bottle of poison. All those things were eventually thrown into a quarry to get rid of them. Sullivan thought at first of donating them to the Historical Society but then he said no, why expose people to all those bad memories.[89]

A little more than a decade after the Oker and Johnson murders, Chief Sullivan destroyed most of the evidence in the Rockport Police's possession. Only some evidence remained—Ada Johnson's blackened eyeglasses, a tuft of her hair and the shard of her skull found in her hallway. No paperwork or photographs from these unsolved cases survive in Rockport—only a few ghoulish artifacts squirreled away in a strongbox.

That strongbox is rumored to still be at the Rockport Police Station.

At least a dozen books have been published on the Lizzie Borden murder trial in Fall River. Writers have devoted articles, plays and even cartoon segments of *The Simpsons* to the case. In 2015, the CEO of the Fall River Chamber of Commerce estimated that fifty-four thousand tourists visit the Borden house each year. Lizzie Borden may have given her mother forty whacks, but she gave her city something more substantial: a tourist economy perpetual motion machine. Fall River, frankly, cannot stop talking about Lizzie Borden.

By contrast, Rockport says nothing—at least to outsiders—about its two equally violent and unsolved murders. Locals have long spoken in elliptical hints. Rockport historian Eleanor Parsons said she knew who committed the crimes and had considered writing a book but decided against it, lest she expose herself to retribution. Bradley Smith speculated the murderer was a man who had immigrated with Oker back in 1904 and then killed him after a theological argument. Both Smith and Parsons hinted there were "smuggler's tunnels" underneath Rockport where the killer hid and where the weapon could be found. Rockport barber Walter Julian succinctly commented, "I could tell you who killed them, but I won't."

The murderer? No one knows *or can prove* who he was. Only one thing seems certain. As this century began, former Rockport Police Chief J. Tom McCarthy speculated that the killer is probably *dead*.

EPILOGUE

My grandfather's murder had changed an entire way of life in Rockport. The town had formerly been a community of trust and honesty among its entire citizenry and doors were never locked. But after this murder things changed. Neighbors looked at one another and couldn't help but be nervous and doors were now locked tight and shades drawn at night....It didn't take a Sherlock Holmes or a Perry Mason to figure out that whoever committed both murders still lived in town and was known to all. Needless to say this caused terrible pressures within the community, as everyone scrambled to establish alibis for the night of this second murder. There are still people in town who will not speak about those days when a large number of State Troopers were barracked in the Town Hall and went through every house in town searching for clues and finding none.[90]

Essex Country voters re-elected Cregg for district attorney in 1934, one of the few Massachusetts Republicans to survive an otherwise Democratic landslide. The voters kept re-electing him. In 1958, the old veteran was finally defeated by Democrat John P.S. Burke, who railed against Cregg's partial residence in Florida, some $300 worth of long-distance phone calls and the twenty-nine unsolved murders during his twenty-eight-year tenure. Cregg died soon after leaving office and is now most remembered for being the grandfather of rock star Huey Lewis.

Cregg didactically expressed his philosophy: "What we need is a little more fireplace, more family gatherings, and more family talk. We must teach the young fellows that happiness is only gained by living a decent life, with a clear conscience and a clean heart, and having more religion."

State Detective Lieutenant William Murray died in early June 1941. His partner, Detective Griffin, was one of the pallbearers at his funeral. Griffin retired in 1945 and died in 1970.

Officer James Quinn retired from the Rockport Police in 1944 after sixteen years of service, becoming a railroad engineer and then a security guard. He died in 1975 after his leg was amputated as a result of diabetes, never having fulfilled his vow to catch the Rockport Maniac.

His hair turning silver, Ernest Thorsell became the department chaplain for the Massachusetts State Police.

August Olson continued as chairman of the SCC in the mid-1930s. His reputation as a master granite carver grew over the subsequent decades, as he carved the sea-green fountains at Union Station Plaza in Washington, D.C., and other monument works as far away as Chicago. He died in 1968, with his services held at the Burgess Funeral Home. *Gloucester Daily Times* correspondent and Cape Ann granite historian Barbara Erkkila commented in his obituary that Olson always "kept his hammers sharp and ready."

Warren Olson remained active in the SCC, eventually becoming head of the Sunday school and a trustee. In the early 1940s, he moved to Cambridge, joined the U.S. Naval Reserves during World War II and retired from the navy after thirty-one years of service. He then became a research chemist for Lever Brothers. Retiring to South Carolina, he died in 2005 at the age of ninety-one.

Former pastor Waldemar Harrald continued living at the Sailor's Home in East Boston. He kept in touch with the SCC congregants, giving a guest sermon in 1936 and visiting the Olson family in 1944.

Albert Johanson served as pastor of the SCC till the mid-1930s and then moved on, with his movements difficult to trace. His wife, Helen, died in Sag Harbor, New York, in 1953. The reverend died in 1968 in Irvington-on-Hudson, New York.

The Swedish Congregational Church, with August Olson as chairman, continued, with former pastor Oscar F. Johnson resuming his post at the church in 1936 and Ida Oker still volunteering on the flower committee for the Ladies Aid Society. Due to the church's declining membership, in 1948, the congregation sold the church building at 111 Granite Street to Norwegian arctic explorer William Knudsen. In 1953, Ms. Katherine Foster, head social worker for the Hospital School for Crippled Children, purchased

Epilogue

the building as a summer home. It has since passed into other hands as a private residence.

The Oker family continued to live in Rockport. Rudy Oker and Captain Martin kept the tailor shop going for a while, but eventually, 77 Main Street became a laundromat and, later, an art gallery. Oker's grandson, Rockport historian and town poet laurate Roger Martin published several books on Rockport history, which included recollections of the Oker-Johnson cases. At the request of Martin's daughter, in the 1990s, he contacted the Massachusetts State Police to find the file on the Oker case. The state police found the case file.

They found it empty.[91]

Rockport Finns have never completely forgotten the murders. Fred Peterson was born after the Oker-Johnson cases, but as he put it during a 2024 interview, "We rarely talked about these crimes, really only when some visitor new to Rockport came by and they were interested." There were many visitors, however, because Fred grew up in his family's house on Hillside Road, known among local Finns as "the Halfway House" because of its location midway between Cape Ann's two Lutheran churches, St. Paul in Lanesville and St. Paul's in Rockport. According to Fred, the house welcomed anyone who was walking the shortcut through the woods either to or from church services.

"Visitors were frequent in our kitchen for coffee and nisu every Sunday," he recalled. Sometimes the locals brought visitors from outside, even Finland. Fred thus heard a couple of things about the investigation repeatedly.

Fred and Joanne Peterson, 2024. *Facebook.*

"First, my grandfather, Antti Kokkonen, or Andrew Kokkonen, was interviewed for hours by the Rockport Police as if he were a suspect," Fred said. "Because he was fit and healthy, and even in his seventies being a strong man, he could not be excluded."

Before quarryman's lung from his exposure to stone dust killed him in late 1933, Antti, a broad-backed and muscular man, had come to America. He was exceptionally skilled, having already worked in soapstone quarries over in Finland and as a blacksmith. Antti trained and supervised crews who worked the king's and queen's quarries before the granite industry shut down and men were idled by the Depression. "The police may have hoped that he had heard and knew something from one of the twenty or so men he had once supervised and kept in contact with. But he knew nothing and had no connection to the murders."

Fred added, "Second—although this was not unique with our family—I heard that the entire fifteen rooms of our house were searched. That meant no privacy for the seven family members living in the house at that time. Nothing that would happen today."

NOTES

Chapter 1

1. Gloucester City Directory, 1932.

Chapter 2

2. Memories of Honorable H. Lawrence Jodrey (anecdote about Chief Sullivan), in *Rockport Remembered*, 53. Jodrey names the complainant and calls her a "trouble maker," so this citation omits her name.

Chapter 3

3. The other two Swedish churches were Lutheran, located on Pigeon Hill Street and later Stockholm Avenue, and Methodist, located on Granite Street. The Lutheran church was the most conservative, affiliated with Swedish aristocracy; the Methodist was more middle of the road. The Congregational Church's 50th Anniversary Historical Sketch took a swipe at their fellow immigrants with the comment, "The Lutherans were strong in their loyalty to the church of their fathers and had difficulty in sympathizing with the free movement." Rockport historian Reinhold L. Swan pointed out that this fragmenting result "was ultimately accomplished, but not we suspect without some disturbing social effects." See Swan, *Swedish Element*.
4. "Short History," 1932, 4–5, PDF scan of typewritten SCC report, Brandel Library, North Park University Archives.
5. "Closing In," *Boston Post*.

Chapter 5

6. Contemporary newspaper accounts do not document when Linder left Oker's store. It is probable that he left before the postman arrived and that one of the two men the mailman saw in the shop was Linder.
7. The MSP investigation file states Dorothy saw the straw-hatted man trying the front door at a little after 11:00 a.m. The newspapers did not identify Dorothy but reported her seeing the man exit the shop's front door sometime after noon, walking with his head bowed, preventing identification.
8. Synopsis by Detective Murray of Ralph Wilson's witness statement, MSP investigative report, June 13, 1932.
9. Rudolph told investigators that he walked up Main Street, looking in several businesses, including the Smith Hardware Store, presumably at 17 Railroad Avenue, which would have been roughly a ten-minute walk.

Chapter 8

10. "Rockport Man Beaten to Death," *Boston Herald*.
11. By this point, Officer Allen, who had accompanied Oker to Addison Gilbert Hospital, was back at 77 Main Street. He presumably rode with the body to the Burgess Funeral Home and then returned to Oker's shop.
12. See footnote on the witness statement from Mrs. Dorothy.

Chapter 9

13. "Appeal to Public," *Boston Herald*. That day, the *Gloucester Daily Times* reported it was the largest funeral in SCC history.

Chapter 10

14. "Lottery Charge," *Gloucester Daily Times*; "Fine for Having Lottery Tickets," *Gloucester Daily Times*. At the time, there were three "Henry Hendricksons" on Cape Ann: two from Rockport and one from Gloucester. The latter was likely the arrested individual, who was being investigated by Gloucester detectives for selling lottery tickets to people on the city's relief rolls.
15. One of the men arrested was Rockport resident William Hendrickson, who was "coming from Gloucester with a gallon of moonshine and rand away to conceal the police discovering it." Source: MSP investigation file.
16. "Now Feel Murderer," *Boston Post*; "Rockport Man Slain," *Gloucester Daily Times*.
17. "Officials Baffled," *Gloucester Daily Times*.
18. "Rockport Man Beaten to Death," *Boston Herald*.

NOTES TO PAGES 47–65

19. "Now Feel Murderer," *Boston Post*.
20. "Officials Baffled," *Gloucester Daily Times*. The article stated, in part, "There was also the rumor that he had won $1,100 in a lottery pool, although this story spread rapidly, there is positively no foundation for such statement."
21. "Seek Lottery Agent," *Boston Herald*.
22. "Appeal to Public," *Boston Herald*.
23. "Officials Baffled," *Gloucester Daily Times*.
24. "Now Feel Murderer," *Boston Post*.
25. "Rockport Crime Remains," *Gloucester Daily Times*.
26. "Murder Case Baffles," *Gloucester Daily Times*.
27. The MSP investigation file lists witness "Melvin Olson" as living at 249 Eastern Avenue but does not specify which town—Gloucester or Rockport. The 1929–30 Gloucester City Directory does not list a Melvin Olson. It is possible this "Melvin Olson" is the Harvard-bound brother of Warren Olson of Oakland Avenue.
28. "Report No New Development," *Gloucester Daily Times*.

Chapter 11

29. Mass General Law, Part IV, Title II, Chapter 276, §10 permits town selectmen or aldermen to post a $500 reward for information on a person who has committed a felony violation in that town.
30. MSP investigative report, June 13, 1932.

Chapter 12

31. "Charge Rockport Selectman," *Gloucester Daily Times*.
32. "Parker Replies," *Gloucester Daily Times*.
33. SCC Pastors Annual Report, 1932, PDF scan, Brandel Library, North Park University Archives.
34. SCC Short History, 1932, PDF scan, Brandel Library, North Park University Archives.

Chapter 13

35. "Man Reveals," *Boston Traveler*.

Chapter 14

36. This sequence seems likely; August would drop everyone else off in the car first and then drop Ada last, since the Olsons and the Johnsons lived across the street

from each other. It follows then that he'd ask Warren to go back to the party and drive other guests home.
37. "Robber Kills Rich Widow," *Boston American*; "Troopers to Attend Rites," *Boston Herald*. In the *Herald* article, August stated he put the car in the garage and made no mention of Warren picking up any remaining party guests.

Chapter 18

38. "Widow Slain," *Boston Post*.
39. "Troopers to Search," *Boston Post*.
40. "Widow's Pastor Called," *Boston Traveler*.
41. "Grill Deranged Man," *Boston Globe*.
42. Newspapers reported the man's name as Otto Erickson, but no one by that name is listed in the 1930 Rockport City Directory. It was possibly Gustav Erickson, who lived at 112 Granite Street, a half mile from Ada's house.
43. "Closing In," *Boston Post*.
44. "Widow Slain," *Boston Post*.
45. Reverend Johnson told the *Lynn Daily Item* that he was at a church event but told the *Boston Traveler* he went to a theatrical party.
46. "Widow's Pastor Called," *Boston Traveler*; "Unbalanced Man Sought," *Lynn Daily Item*.
47. "Man Reveals," *Boston Traveler*.
48. "Widow's Slayer Hid," *Boston Post*.
49. "Attack on Pastor," *Boston American*.
50. "Murder Laid to Neighbor," *Boston Globe*.
51. "Seek 'Nudist Spy,'" *Boston Daily Record*.
52. "Cavern Under Haunted House," *Boston Post*.
53. "Prosecutors However Admit Slow Progress," *Gloucester Daily Times*. The article implies that the crime scene became tainted in the efforts to get Oker to the hospital. Selectman Parker's December 19, 1932 op-ed letter specifically states that the police let the public enter the crime scene after the attack. Martin, *Rockport Recollected*, 113. "The State police pulled the fingerprints of the entire Rockport police force at the crime scene." Given the circumstances of the attack and the inexperience of the Rockport Police in murder cases, it is probable that the crime scene was contaminated.
54. "Arrest Nearer," *Boston Globe*.
55. "Arrest Nearer," *Boston Globe*.
56. The precise location of the "Babson Farm" was not recorded in contemporary accounts. It is possible that the building was the Norwood House (aka Old Farm Inn) on Granite Street near Halibut Point.

57. "Suspect Clew Proves Futile," *Boston Globe*, November 7, 1933.
58. "Police in Conference for Hours," *Gloucester Daily Times*.
59. "Raided Larder," *Boston Globe*.
60. "Two More Detectives and Four Troopers," *Gloucester Daily Times*.

CHAPTER 19

61. "Combing Rockport," *Gloucester Daily Times*.
62. "New Rockport Death," *Boston American*.
63. "Police Split," *Boston Traveler*.
64. "Police Split," *Boston Traveler*.
65. "Police Split," *Boston Traveler*.
66. "Trooper in Pulpit Asks," *Boston Daily Record*; see also, "Gen Needham Satisfied," *Boston Globe*; "Officer Becomes Preacher," *Boston Globe*; "Police-Pastor in Pulpit," *Boston Herald*.
67. "Tarr Defends Boy," *Boston Daily Record*; "Widow Killing Clues," *Boston Sunday Advertiser*; "Killer May Walk Streets," *Boston Sunday Post*; Martin, *Rockport Remembered*, 146; "Who Killed?" *Boston Globe*. Local lore has it that Ada mentioned knowing the identity of the killer at the Halloween party, and she stated the person should turn themselves in or she would go to the police. The 1933 newspaper articles state only that she knew or suspected who the killer was.
68. "Olson Charges Police," *Boston Globe*.
69. "Trooper-Preacher in Pulpit," *Gloucester Daily Times*.
70. "Norwood Youths Grilled," *Gloucester Daily Times*.
71. Probably just as well. Dr. Hickson, the "Chicago psycopathist," was a published eugenicist who blamed women's suffrage for turning American men into "sissies" and the United Sates into a "jelly-bean nation." See Hickson, "What Will You Be?"
72. "Olson Charges Police," *Boston Globe*.
73. "Olson Charges Police," *Boston Globe*.
74. "Foreclosure Gives Clue," *Boston Herald*. The paper did not specify which foreclosure notice was of interest to the investigators. Our research in the Salem deeds database uncovered no records in the index for Rockport Granite Savings Bank and Rockport National Bank for November 15, 1933, the article dateline. Note that the date a real estate transaction is filed may not be the same date that it is recorded. We searched for last names mentioned in our story, but no luck. Scores of foreclosures were filed in 1933—it was the Depression, after all—so this avenue is the proverbial search for a needle in a haystack.
75. For details on rumrunning in Rockport, see the recollections of Robert Rapp, Cynthia Peckham and David C. Waddell in *Rockport Remembered*, 76, 123–24, 126.

NOTES TO PAGES 137–159

CHAPTER 20

76. "New Angle in Probe," *Boston Post*.
77. "Detective Out of Fiction Needed," *Boston Globe*.
78. "Detective Out of Fiction Needed," *Boston Globe*.
79. "Officer Spoke," *Gloucester Daily Times*.

CHAPTER 21

80. "Link Killings," *Boston Post*.

CHAPTER 22

81. "Slaughter of Animals," *Boston Globe*.

CHAPTER 23

82. "Police Seek Prowler," *Gloucester Daily Times*.
83. "Says Girls Assailant," *Boston Post*.
84. "Officer Investigates Yarn," *Gloucester Daily Times*.
85. MSP investigative report, June 14, 1938.
86. "Trio Set Upon Officer," *Gloucester Daily Times*.
87. See "Bookmakers Turn Gangster," *Boston Evening Transcript*, which mentions that most Massachusetts murders in previous decade had origins in gambling rackets.

CHAPTER 24

88. Citing a transcription by Rockporter Harry Wheeler for the WPA's American Life Histories project, in Martin, *Rockport Recollected*; see also Library of Congress, "U.S. Work Projects Administration, Federal Writers' Project, Folklore Project, Life Histories, 1936–39, [Gor Svenson #4]."
89. Martin, *Rockport Remembered*, 51.

EPILOGUE

90. Martin, *Rockport Recollected*, 72–73.
91. Thanks to the efforts of the Records Division of the Massachusetts State Police, the authors were able to obtain twenty-one scanned pages from the Oker investigation, with document dates between 1932 and 1945. However, the Records Division was unable to locate any files from the Ada Johnson case.

BIBLIOGRAPHY

Books

East, Elyssa. *Dogtown: Death and Enchantment in a New England Ghost Town*. New York: Simon & Schuster Books, 2010.

Erkkila, Betty Anne (Kielinen). *My Little Chickadee, Coming of Age in the 1940s & 1950s Rockport, Massachusetts*. Self-published; prepress by North Star Press of St. Cloud Inc., 2011.

Erkkila, John W., and Betty Anne (Kielinen) Erkkila. *Souvenirs of Pigeon Cove*. Self-published; prepress by North Star Press of St. Cloud Inc., 2014.

Martin, Roger. *Rockport Recollected: Real Stories from Real People*. Gloucester, MA: Curious Traveler Press, 2001.

———. *Rockport Remembered: An Oral History*. Gloucester, MA: Curious Traveler Press, 1997.

O'Malley, Dr. Patricia Trainor. *The Irish in Haverhill, Massachusetts*. Vol. 2. Charleston, SC: Arcadia Publishing, 1999.

Powers, William F. *French and Electric Blue; The Massachusetts State Police*. Lowell, MA: Sullivan Brothers, 1980.

Swan, Marshall. W.S. *Town on Sandy Bay*. Canaan, NH: Phoenix Publishing, 1980.

City and Town Publications

Gloucester City Directories, 1932, 1935.
Rockport City Directory, 1929–30.
Town of Rockport Annual Report, 1933, 1934.

Bibliography

Pamphlets

Swan, Reinhold L. *The Swedish Element on Cape Ann, 1880–1900.* Rockport Public Library, 1966.

Scanned Materials

Swedish Mission, Pigeon Cove, MA. Church materials—reports, histories. 1918–48. Box: 4, folder: 5. Dissolved or Disbanded Covenant Church Records, 8–16. Evangelical Covenant Church, North Park University Archives.

State Police Records

Massachusetts Responsive Record of Investigation files 1932-45. Public Record Request #P006441-082823 (21 pages).

Websites

Boston Globe. H. Lawrence Jodrey Obituary. June 26, 2004. https://www.legacy.com/us/obituaries/bostonglobe/name/h-jodrey-obituary?id=27072396.

Day, Reverend Paul. "On the Move: 125 Years of the East Coast Conference." East Coast Conference. 2016 http://eastcoastconf.org/wp-content/uploads/2016/05/125th-Anniversary-History-of-the-East-Coast-Conference.pdf.

eBay. "Photograph of Reverend Thorsell." https://www.ebay.com/itm/353160954761.

FBI: UCR. "Crime in the United States 2011." https://ucr.fbi.gov/crime-in-the-u.s/2011/crime-in-the-u.s.-2011/offenses-known-to-law-enforcement/expanded/expanded-homicide-data.

Flying Tiger Antiques. "Rare 1957 Massachusetts State Police Credentials for Dept. Chaplain Ernest A. Thorsell." https://www.flyingtigerantiques.com/rare-1957-massachusetts-state-police-credentials-for-dept-chaplain-ernest-a-thorsell.html.

Greenville News. Warren Olson Obituary. April 23, 2005. https://www.legacy.com/us/obituaries/greenvilleonline/name/warren-olson-obituary?id=48978513.

Hickson, Dr. William J. "What Will You Be? A Man or a Jelly Bean? Shall America Collapse from Effeminacy? 'It's Up to You, Son!'" https://newseumed.org/sites/default/files/legacy/2015/09/WST-NAOWS_01.pdf.

Library of Congress. "U.S. Work Projects Administration, Federal Writers' Project, Folklore Project, Life Histories, 1936–39, [Gor Svenson #4]." https://www.loc.gov/item/wpalh000723/.

Bibliography

Massachusetts State Police Museum and Learning Center. "Joseph Louis Ferrari." Facebook. July 7, 2020. https://www.facebook.com/MSPMLC/photos/joseph-louis-ferrari-giuseppe-luigi-ferrari-was-born-in-boston-on-february-5-188/4646784985347766/.

Minnesota Digital Library. "Wedding Portrait of Reverend Albert Johanson with His Wife, Duluth Minnesota." https://collection.mndigital.org/catalog/p16022coll20:36#?c=&m=&s=&cv=&xywh=-2329%2C-87%2C8404%2C5239.

Rockport Town Directories. www.ancestry.com.

Salem Registry of Deeds. https://www.salemdeeds.com/salemdeeds/Default2.aspx.

Scott, Courtney. "Rockport's Murder Mystery: Going to the Grave." Medium. May 10, 2015. https://medium.com/@coscott15/rockport-s-murder-mystery-going-to-the-grave-90424612b9d8.

Vintage Rockport. www.vintagerockport.com.

Wikipedia. "Hugh Cregg." https://en.wikipedia.org/wiki/Hugh_Cregg.

Newspaper Articles

Boston American (also *Boston Advertiser* and *Boston Evening American*). "Attack Linked in Killing." November 20, 1933.

———. "Attack on Pastor—Fingerprint Clues—In Rockport Slaying," November 4, 1933.

———. "Cattle Slaughter Seen as Clue to Rockport Maniac." November 4, 1934.

———. "Churchman in Rockport to Face Grill." November 17, 1933.

———. "Francis Cochran Had Date With a 'Man She Didn't Like.'" September 28, 1942.

———. "Friendship Is Murder Clue." May 26, 1932.

———. "Hammer Death Clues Fail." October 23, 1934.

———. "Hammer Probe Turns Here." October 20, 1934.

———. "Killer Hunt Is Begun in Church." November 2, 1933.

———. "Left-Handed Man Sought as Slayer." November 4, 1933.

———. "New Rockport Death Mystery Bared." November 10, 1933.

———. "New Rockport Slayer Hunt." May 31, 1932.

———. "Olson Story Gives Police Killing Clue." November 5, 1933.

———. "Robber Kills Rich Widow, Burns Body." November 1, 1933.

———. "Rockport Boy, 7, Hurt by Fall." March 23, 1938.

———. "Rockport's Hammer Crime: Police Grill Five Suspects." October 19, 1934.

———. "Salesmen Held in Oker Death." May 28, 1932.

———. "Stonecutter Hunted as Slayer." November 4, 1933.

———. "Tarr Protests Kidnapping in Rockport Death Quiz." November 14, 1933.

———. "Torch Killer Is Linked to Attack on Pastor." November 3, 1933.

———. "Trio Linked in Slaying at Rockport." November 7, 1933.

Bibliography

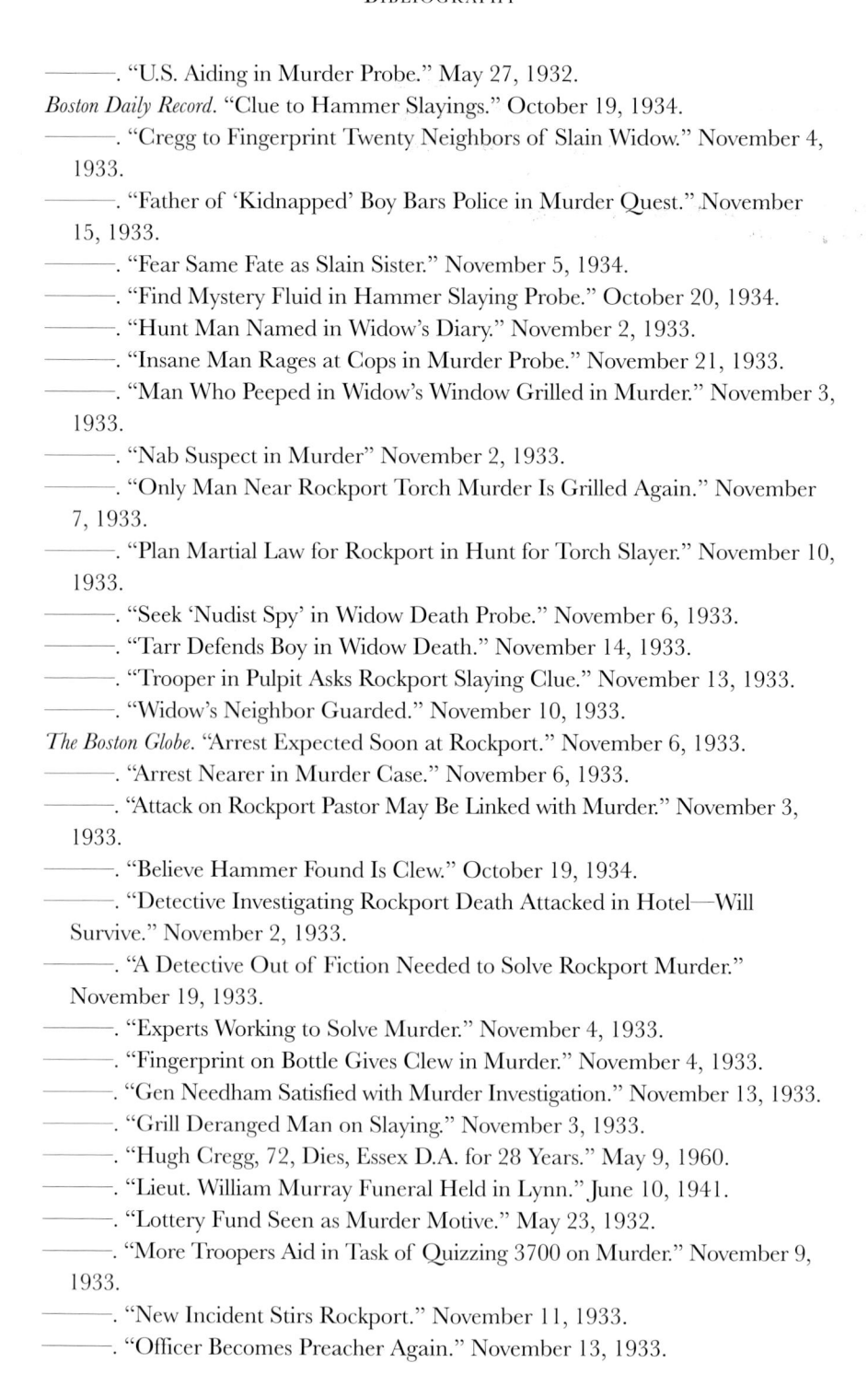

———. "U.S. Aiding in Murder Probe." May 27, 1932.

Boston Daily Record. "Clue to Hammer Slayings." October 19, 1934.

———. "Cregg to Fingerprint Twenty Neighbors of Slain Widow." November 4, 1933.

———. "Father of 'Kidnapped' Boy Bars Police in Murder Quest." November 15, 1933.

———. "Fear Same Fate as Slain Sister." November 5, 1934.

———. "Find Mystery Fluid in Hammer Slaying Probe." October 20, 1934.

———. "Hunt Man Named in Widow's Diary." November 2, 1933.

———. "Insane Man Rages at Cops in Murder Probe." November 21, 1933.

———. "Man Who Peeped in Widow's Window Grilled in Murder." November 3, 1933.

———. "Nab Suspect in Murder" November 2, 1933.

———. "Only Man Near Rockport Torch Murder Is Grilled Again." November 7, 1933.

———. "Plan Martial Law for Rockport in Hunt for Torch Slayer." November 10, 1933.

———. "Seek 'Nudist Spy' in Widow Death Probe." November 6, 1933.

———. "Tarr Defends Boy in Widow Death." November 14, 1933.

———. "Trooper in Pulpit Asks Rockport Slaying Clue." November 13, 1933.

———. "Widow's Neighbor Guarded." November 10, 1933.

The Boston Globe. "Arrest Expected Soon at Rockport." November 6, 1933.

———. "Arrest Nearer in Murder Case." November 6, 1933.

———. "Attack on Rockport Pastor May Be Linked with Murder." November 3, 1933.

———. "Believe Hammer Found Is Clew." October 19, 1934.

———. "Detective Investigating Rockport Death Attacked in Hotel—Will Survive." November 2, 1933.

———. "A Detective Out of Fiction Needed to Solve Rockport Murder." November 19, 1933.

———. "Experts Working to Solve Murder." November 4, 1933.

———. "Fingerprint on Bottle Gives Clew in Murder." November 4, 1933.

———. "Gen Needham Satisfied with Murder Investigation." November 13, 1933.

———. "Grill Deranged Man on Slaying." November 3, 1933.

———. "Hugh Cregg, 72, Dies, Essex D.A. for 28 Years." May 9, 1960.

———. "Lieut. William Murray Funeral Held in Lynn." June 10, 1941.

———. "Lottery Fund Seen as Murder Motive." May 23, 1932.

———. "More Troopers Aid in Task of Quizzing 3700 on Murder." November 9, 1933.

———. "New Incident Stirs Rockport." November 11, 1933.

———. "Officer Becomes Preacher Again." November 13, 1933.

Bibliography

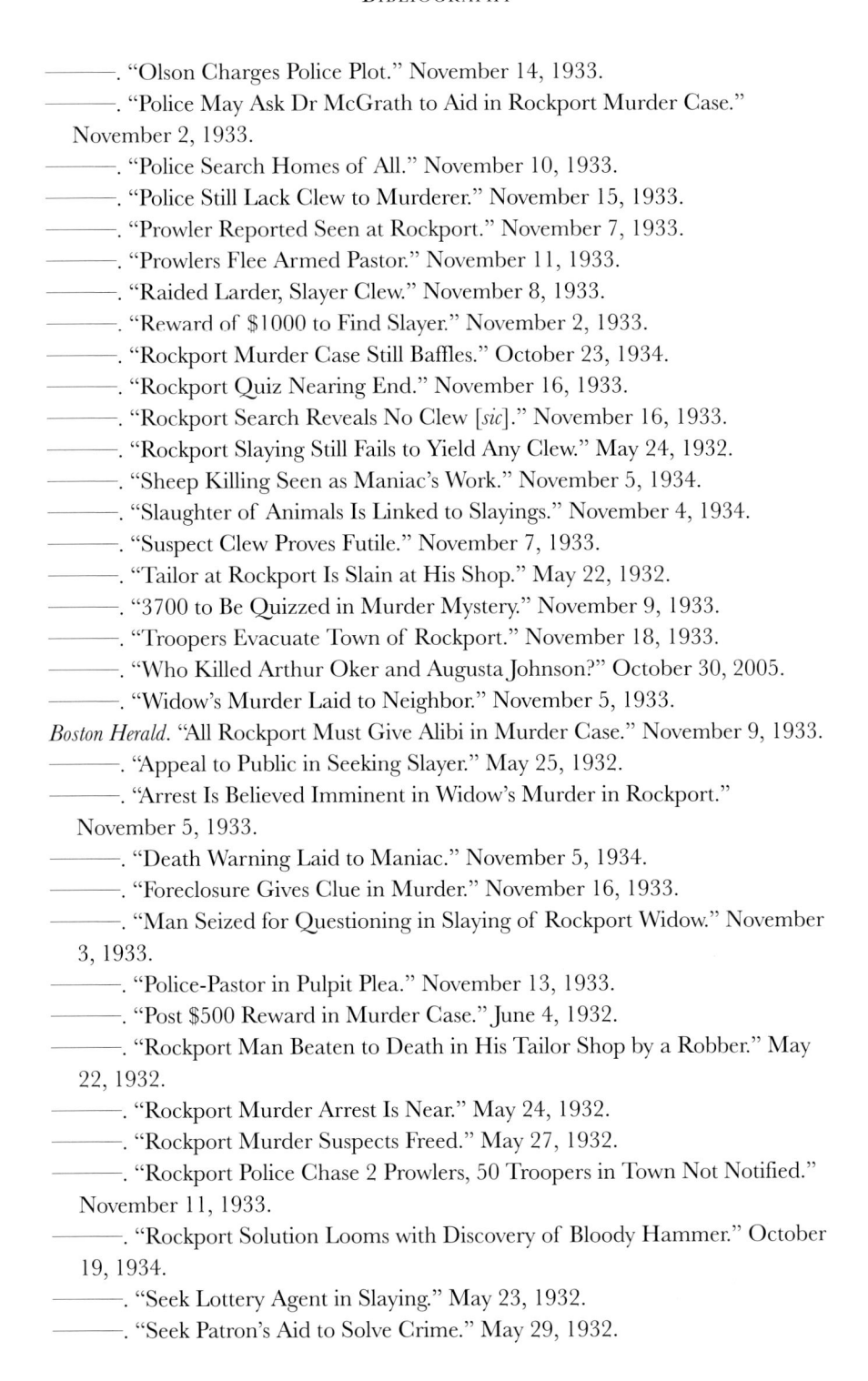

———. "Olson Charges Police Plot." November 14, 1933.
———. "Police May Ask Dr McGrath to Aid in Rockport Murder Case." November 2, 1933.
———. "Police Search Homes of All." November 10, 1933.
———. "Police Still Lack Clew to Murderer." November 15, 1933.
———. "Prowler Reported Seen at Rockport." November 7, 1933.
———. "Prowlers Flee Armed Pastor." November 11, 1933.
———. "Raided Larder, Slayer Clew." November 8, 1933.
———. "Reward of $1000 to Find Slayer." November 2, 1933.
———. "Rockport Murder Case Still Baffles." October 23, 1934.
———. "Rockport Quiz Nearing End." November 16, 1933.
———. "Rockport Search Reveals No Clew [*sic*]." November 16, 1933.
———. "Rockport Slaying Still Fails to Yield Any Clew." May 24, 1932.
———. "Sheep Killing Seen as Maniac's Work." November 5, 1934.
———. "Slaughter of Animals Is Linked to Slayings." November 4, 1934.
———. "Suspect Clew Proves Futile." November 7, 1933.
———. "Tailor at Rockport Is Slain at His Shop." May 22, 1932.
———. "3700 to Be Quizzed in Murder Mystery." November 9, 1933.
———. "Troopers Evacuate Town of Rockport." November 18, 1933.
———. "Who Killed Arthur Oker and Augusta Johnson?" October 30, 2005.
———. "Widow's Murder Laid to Neighbor." November 5, 1933.
Boston Herald. "All Rockport Must Give Alibi in Murder Case." November 9, 1933.
———. "Appeal to Public in Seeking Slayer." May 25, 1932.
———. "Arrest Is Believed Imminent in Widow's Murder in Rockport." November 5, 1933.
———. "Death Warning Laid to Maniac." November 5, 1934.
———. "Foreclosure Gives Clue in Murder." November 16, 1933.
———. "Man Seized for Questioning in Slaying of Rockport Widow." November 3, 1933.
———. "Police-Pastor in Pulpit Plea." November 13, 1933.
———. "Post $500 Reward in Murder Case." June 4, 1932.
———. "Rockport Man Beaten to Death in His Tailor Shop by a Robber." May 22, 1932.
———. "Rockport Murder Arrest Is Near." May 24, 1932.
———. "Rockport Murder Suspects Freed." May 27, 1932.
———. "Rockport Police Chase 2 Prowlers, 50 Troopers in Town Not Notified." November 11, 1933.
———. "Rockport Solution Looms with Discovery of Bloody Hammer." October 19, 1934.
———. "Seek Lottery Agent in Slaying." May 23, 1932.
———. "Seek Patron's Aid to Solve Crime." May 29, 1932.

BIBLIOGRAPHY

———. "Seek Stranger in Murder Case." November 6, 1933.
———. "State Troopers to Attend Rites for Rockport Victim." November 4, 1933.
———. "Unique House to House Probe Opened in Rockport Murder." November 10, 1933.
———. "Wide Hunt for Rockport Slayer Launched as $1000 Is Offered." November 2, 1933.
Boston Post. "Boy Beaten Left as Dead in Rockport." March 23, 1938.
———. "Cavern Under Haunted House Clue to Killer." November 6, 1933.
———. "Closing In on Cape Ann Killer." November 4, 1933.
———. "Find Marks Not Prints of Slayer." November 10, 1933.
———. "Fingerprints Clue to Murderer at Rockport." November 2, 1933.
———. "Hunt for Rockport Prowler." November 11, 1933.
———. "Kidnapping Blamed on Troopers." November 14, 1933.
———. "Link Killings in Rockport." October 23, 1934.
———. "Link Laughter to Old Crimes." March 1, 1936.
———. "Mystery Man Seen as Killer." May 24, 1932.
———. "New Angle in Probe of Slayings." November 17, 1933.
———. "New Clue to Double Murderer." October 19, 1934.
———. "New Light on Murder Case." May 25, 1932.
———. "No Sleep After Oker Killing." November 21, 1933.
———. "Now Feel Murderer a Local Man." May 23, 1932.
———. "Officials Baffled in Search for Murderer." November 7, 1933.
———. "Plan Study of Revenge Clue." November 16, 1933.
———. "Quiz Bookie in Murder of Taylor." December 14, 1939.
———. "Quiz Man Who Cared for Estate." November 18, 1933.
———. "Ring Found in Murder Home Ruins." November 12, 1933.
———. "Rockport Killer May Walk Streets of Town Still." September 7, 1941.
———. "Says Girls Assailant Murderer." September 23, 1936.
———. "Slain for $1200 Won in a Pool." May 22, 1932.
———. "State Troopers to Search 100 Homes." November 9, 1933.
———. "Think Widow's Slayer Hid for Hours." November 5, 1933.
———. "Uniformed Man Sought as Slayer." May 27, 1932.
———. "Widow Slain by Spurned Suitor." November 3, 1933.
———. "Year 1933 Filled with Many Unsolved Mysterious Murders." January 1, 1934.
Boston Sunday Advertiser. "Dead Woman's Nuptial Ring Is Found in Debris of Home." November 12, 1933.
———. "Widow Killing Clues Blasted." November 19, 1933.
Boston Transcript. "Bookmakers Turn Gangster to Raise Wager Payments." December 13, 1939.
———. "3700 Must Get Alibis in Rockport Murder." November 9, 1933.

Bibliography

Boston Traveler. "Church Members Hunt Rockport Widow Killer." November 2, 1933.
———. "Friends Face Rockport Grill." November 17, 1933.
———. "Hammer Death Probe Reopens." October 19, 1934.
———. "Police Press Murder Search." October 20, 1934.
———. "Police Split in Rockport." November 11, 1933.
———. "Rockport Armed Camp, Whole Town Questions." November 9, 1933.
———. "Rockport Widow Slain Left to Die in Flames." November 1, 1933.
———. "Slain Widow's Pastor Called." November 3, 1933.
———. "Traveler Man Reveals Rockport Murder Clue." November 4, 1933.
Clinton Daily Item. "Body Found by Firemen." November 1, 1933.
———. "Search Being Conducted." November 2, 1933.
———. "Wholesale Fingerprinting." November 4, 1933.
Fitchburg Sentinel. "Hammer Clue in Rockport Murder Case." October 19, 1934.
———. "Robber Believed to Have Slain Church President." May 23, 1932.
Gloucester Daily Times. "Amputee Says Don't Look Back." April 7, 1975.
———. "Board Rejects Chief's Request to Serve Beyond Retirement." September 10, 1943.
———. "Charge Rockport Selectman with Tipsy Operating." June 13, 1932.
———. "Chief Sullivan Enters Upon His 32nd Term." April 29, 1932.
———. "Citizens Pay Tribute to Long Service of Former Officials." May 16, 1944.
———. "Claim Rockport Officer Refused to Guard Manufacturing Plant." July 16, 1940.
———. "Claims Opponent Not Republican." September 19, 1938.
———. "Combing Rockport for Possible Clues." November 9, 1933.
———. "Final Rehearsal Tonight for Christmas Carol Concert." December 19, 1932.
———. "Find Rockport Boy Unconscious." March 23, 1938.
———. "Fine for Having Lottery Tickets." April 13, 1932.
———. "Former Churches Become Studios Shops and Homes." November 16, 1957.
———. "Four Norwood Youths Grilled by Police." November 14, 1933.
———. "Funeral." February 7, 1968.
———. "Funeral This Afternoon." May 24, 1932.
———. "Green Out as First Assistant in Cregg's Office." April 2, 1935.
———. "Grisly Halloween Murder Still Unsolved After 50 Years." October 31, 1983.
———. "He Carved with an Artist's Touch." February 10, 1968.
———. "History of the Swedish Congregational Church of Pigeon Cove." April 20, 1929.
———. "Hopeful in House to House Canvass." November 10, 1933.
———. "James T. Quinn, 73. Was Rockport Policeman for 17 Years." June 4, 1975.
———. "Killing Sheep and Duck Stirs Up Pigeon Cove." November 5, 1934.
———. Letter to the editor from H. Lawrence Jodrey Jr. October 31, 1942.
———. "Local Man's Sheep Slain—Believed Killed by Dogs." November 9, 1934.

Bibliography

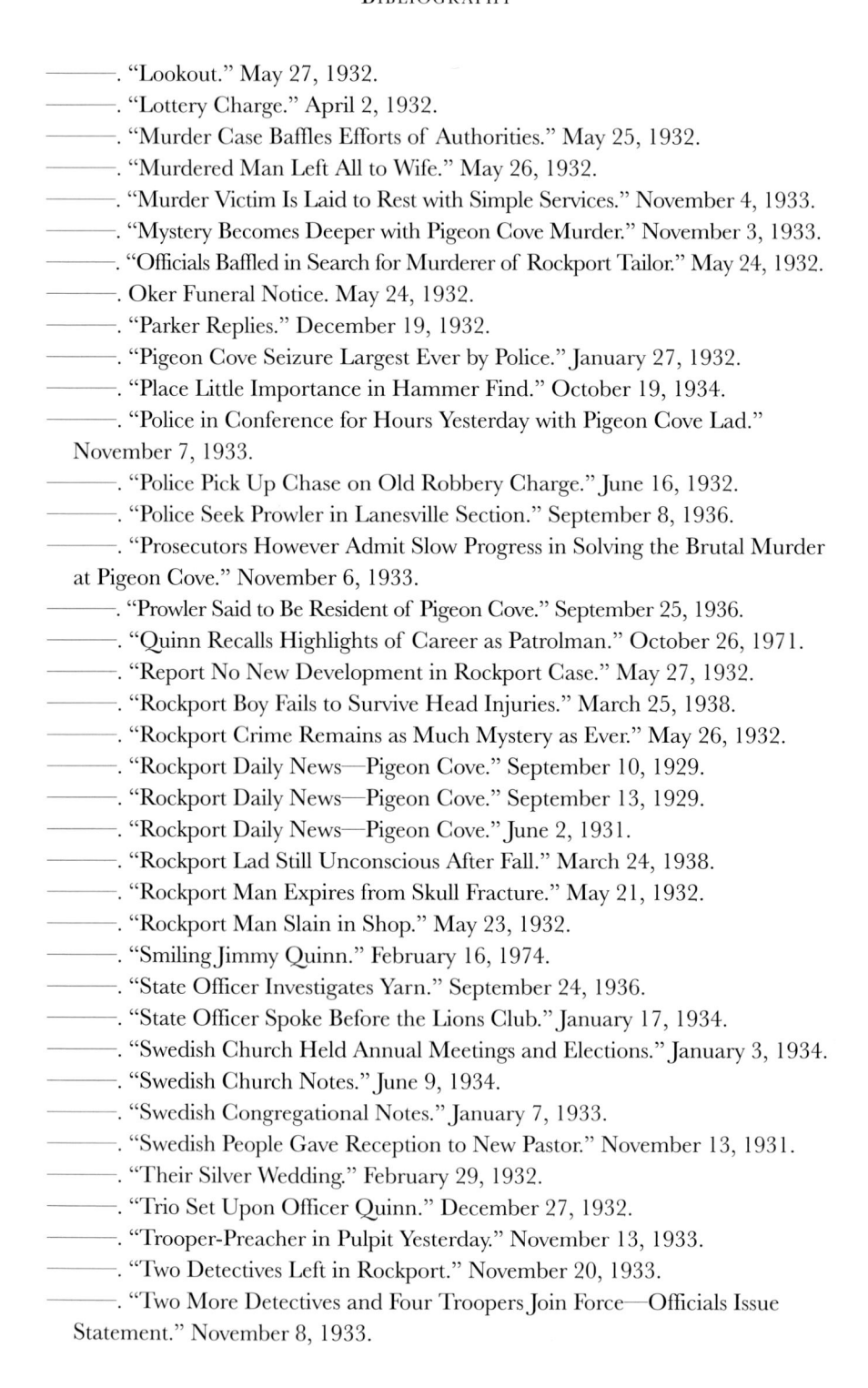

———. "Lookout." May 27, 1932.
———. "Lottery Charge." April 2, 1932.
———. "Murder Case Baffles Efforts of Authorities." May 25, 1932.
———. "Murdered Man Left All to Wife." May 26, 1932.
———. "Murder Victim Is Laid to Rest with Simple Services." November 4, 1933.
———. "Mystery Becomes Deeper with Pigeon Cove Murder." November 3, 1933.
———. "Officials Baffled in Search for Murderer of Rockport Tailor." May 24, 1932.
———. Oker Funeral Notice. May 24, 1932.
———. "Parker Replies." December 19, 1932.
———. "Pigeon Cove Seizure Largest Ever by Police." January 27, 1932.
———. "Place Little Importance in Hammer Find." October 19, 1934.
———. "Police in Conference for Hours Yesterday with Pigeon Cove Lad." November 7, 1933.
———. "Police Pick Up Chase on Old Robbery Charge." June 16, 1932.
———. "Police Seek Prowler in Lanesville Section." September 8, 1936.
———. "Prosecutors However Admit Slow Progress in Solving the Brutal Murder at Pigeon Cove." November 6, 1933.
———. "Prowler Said to Be Resident of Pigeon Cove." September 25, 1936.
———. "Quinn Recalls Highlights of Career as Patrolman." October 26, 1971.
———. "Report No New Development in Rockport Case." May 27, 1932.
———. "Rockport Boy Fails to Survive Head Injuries." March 25, 1938.
———. "Rockport Crime Remains as Much Mystery as Ever." May 26, 1932.
———. "Rockport Daily News—Pigeon Cove." September 10, 1929.
———. "Rockport Daily News—Pigeon Cove." September 13, 1929.
———. "Rockport Daily News—Pigeon Cove." June 2, 1931.
———. "Rockport Lad Still Unconscious After Fall." March 24, 1938.
———. "Rockport Man Expires from Skull Fracture." May 21, 1932.
———. "Rockport Man Slain in Shop." May 23, 1932.
———. "Smiling Jimmy Quinn." February 16, 1974.
———. "State Officer Investigates Yarn." September 24, 1936.
———. "State Officer Spoke Before the Lions Club." January 17, 1934.
———. "Swedish Church Held Annual Meetings and Elections." January 3, 1934.
———. "Swedish Church Notes." June 9, 1934.
———. "Swedish Congregational Notes." January 7, 1933.
———. "Swedish People Gave Reception to New Pastor." November 13, 1931.
———. "Their Silver Wedding." February 29, 1932.
———. "Trio Set Upon Officer Quinn." December 27, 1932.
———. "Trooper-Preacher in Pulpit Yesterday." November 13, 1933.
———. "Two Detectives Left in Rockport." November 20, 1933.
———. "Two More Detectives and Four Troopers Join Force—Officials Issue Statement." November 8, 1933.

Bibliography

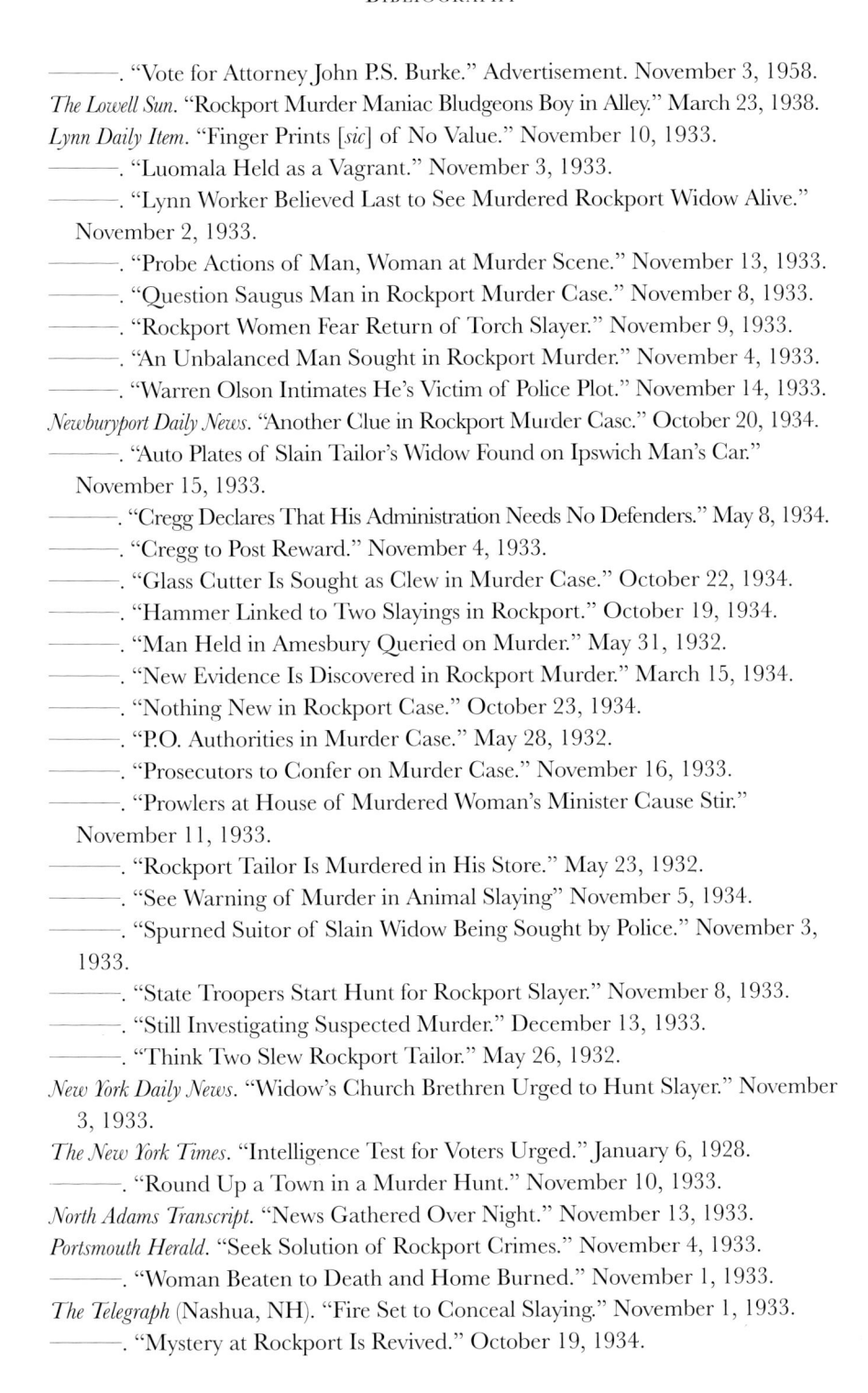

———. "Vote for Attorney John P.S. Burke." Advertisement. November 3, 1958.
The Lowell Sun. "Rockport Murder Maniac Bludgeons Boy in Alley." March 23, 1938.
Lynn Daily Item. "Finger Prints [sic] of No Value." November 10, 1933.
———. "Luomala Held as a Vagrant." November 3, 1933.
———. "Lynn Worker Believed Last to See Murdered Rockport Widow Alive." November 2, 1933.
———. "Probe Actions of Man, Woman at Murder Scene." November 13, 1933.
———. "Question Saugus Man in Rockport Murder Case." November 8, 1933.
———. "Rockport Women Fear Return of Torch Slayer." November 9, 1933.
———. "An Unbalanced Man Sought in Rockport Murder." November 4, 1933.
———. "Warren Olson Intimates He's Victim of Police Plot." November 14, 1933.
Newburyport Daily News. "Another Clue in Rockport Murder Case." October 20, 1934.
———. "Auto Plates of Slain Tailor's Widow Found on Ipswich Man's Car." November 15, 1933.
———. "Cregg Declares That His Administration Needs No Defenders." May 8, 1934.
———. "Cregg to Post Reward." November 4, 1933.
———. "Glass Cutter Is Sought as Clew in Murder Case." October 22, 1934.
———. "Hammer Linked to Two Slayings in Rockport." October 19, 1934.
———. "Man Held in Amesbury Queried on Murder." May 31, 1932.
———. "New Evidence Is Discovered in Rockport Murder." March 15, 1934.
———. "Nothing New in Rockport Case." October 23, 1934.
———. "P.O. Authorities in Murder Case." May 28, 1932.
———. "Prosecutors to Confer on Murder Case." November 16, 1933.
———. "Prowlers at House of Murdered Woman's Minister Cause Stir." November 11, 1933.
———. "Rockport Tailor Is Murdered in His Store." May 23, 1932.
———. "See Warning of Murder in Animal Slaying" November 5, 1934.
———. "Spurned Suitor of Slain Widow Being Sought by Police." November 3, 1933.
———. "State Troopers Start Hunt for Rockport Slayer." November 8, 1933.
———. "Still Investigating Suspected Murder." December 13, 1933.
———. "Think Two Slew Rockport Tailor." May 26, 1932.
New York Daily News. "Widow's Church Brethren Urged to Hunt Slayer." November 3, 1933.
The New York Times. "Intelligence Test for Voters Urged." January 6, 1928.
———. "Round Up a Town in a Murder Hunt." November 10, 1933.
North Adams Transcript. "News Gathered Over Night." November 13, 1933.
Portsmouth Herald. "Seek Solution of Rockport Crimes." November 4, 1933.
———. "Woman Beaten to Death and Home Burned." November 1, 1933.
The Telegraph (Nashua, NH). "Fire Set to Conceal Slaying." November 1, 1933.
———. "Mystery at Rockport Is Revived." October 19, 1934.

During the Oker-Johnson investigations, Rockport children joined the police as volunteers, tagging along wearing metal "Junior Detective" badges and carrying booklets that were given as premiums for box tops by Post Toasties cereals. Here, in 2024, Jayden Soini and Elijah Doucette re-enact badge and booklet bearers at the actual starting site of the mystery, 77 Main Street. *Robert Fitzgibbon.*